Advance praise for *WHEN GOD WALKS AWAY*

Kaye McKee knows the difference between depression and what John of the Cross called *the dark night of the soul.* In this hopeful book, McKee waits patiently through the barren places and finally experiences what she calls "a brilliant darkness," the return of joy and the onset of a new stage of growth. This is a must-read book.

— **Dr. Corinne Ware,** author and professor,
Episcopal Theological Seminary of the Southwest

With elegance and honesty Kaye McKee has given all seekers of light a compelling travel guide for the journey of life. This tear-washed testament is her song in the night, a nocturne to remind us all of this hope: wherever there are shadows, there is also light.

— **Joseph Martin,** composer, recording artist

When *God Walks Away* is a profound expression of Christian hope in the midst of desolation and abandonment. This book is a true companion, as McKee avoids glib answers and invites us to consider the night as one expression of God's longing for us.

— **Dr. David Jensen,** author and professor,
Austin Presbyterian Seminary

I heartily commend *When God Walks Away* to anyone who has experienced the dark night of the soul or who longs to be supportive of any loved one who is in need of wisdom. This is the most helpful book I've read in years, and should be required reading for every therapist.

— **Bob Lively,** author and pastoral counselor

WHEN GOD WALKS AWAY

A Companion for the Journey
Through the Dark Night of the Soul

Kaye P. McKee

A Crossroad Book
The Crossroad Publishing Company
New York

Scripture quotations unless otherwise noted are from the New Revised
Standard Version Bible, copyright © 1989 by the Division of Christian
Education of the National Council of the Churches of Christ in the U.S.A.,
and are used by permission.

The Crossroad Publishing Company
16 Penn Plaza – 481 Eighth Avenue, Suite 1550
New York, NY 10001

Printed in the United States of America

The main text of this book is set in 11/15 Garamond Antiqua; other
text fonts are Goudy Old Style and Optima; the display fonts are Mason,
Calligraphic 810, and Nuptial.

Library of Congress Cataloging-in-Publication Data

McKee, Kaye.
  When God walks away : a companion for the journey through the dark
night of the soul / Kaye McKee.
    p. cm.
  Includes bibliographical references.
  ISBN-13: 978-0-8245-2380-0 (alk. paper)
  ISBN-10: 0-8245-2380-6 (alk. paper)
  1. Hidden God. 2. Mysticism – Psychology. 3. Spiritual formation –
Psychology. 4. Jesus Christ – Passion. 5. Jesus Christ – Resurrection.
6. Suffering – Religious aspects – Christianity. I. Title.
BT180.H54M35 2006
248.8′6 – dc22
                                                            2006013914

1   2   3   4   5   6   7   8   9   10   12   11   10   09   08   07   06

For David, Arielle, and Bethany,
who walked with me through the night

Contents

CHAPTER ONE

THE GREAT ADVENTURE

My God, my God, why have you forsaken me?
Why are you so far from helping me,
from the words of my groaning?
O my God, I cry by day, but you do not answer;
and by night, but find no rest.   —Psalm 22:1–2

That which the anguished soul feels most deeply is the conviction
that God has abandoned it, of which it has no doubt; that He has
cast it away into darkness as an abominable thing....
                                                    —John of the Cross

He has driven and brought me
Into darkness without any light....

My soul is bereft of peace;
I have forgotten what happiness is;
So I say, "Gone is my glory,
And all that I had hoped for from the Lord."

                              —Lamentations 3:2, 17–18

✠ *Why the Night?* ✠

Before the days of sentient thought, before I knew myself as a separate self, I knew God as a sweet and indwelling presence, more real than the rising of the sun or even of my own breath. When our minister visited our home to speak with my older sister about becoming a Christian, I perched on the edge of the sofa, drinking in every word. At last I had a name for the vital relationship in my life. I badgered my parents, who thought me too young to understand Christian commitment, until they relented and I stood, beaming and dripping in the small stone church's baptismal pool. I was eight years old.

Three years later during Sunday worship, our pastor's voice supplied pleasant background music for my practice of counting the bulbs ensconced in the sanctuary's simple chandeliers. In the next moment's breath, I stood in the temple with Isaiah. With the prophet I looked upon the Lord, high and lifted up: the Lord clothed in robes so mammoth, their hem carpeted the temple floor all the way to its farthest corners. Who would not serve such a master as this? And the voice that thrilled in and through me, more real and near than human speech asked, "Whom shall I send and who shall go for us?" And the whole of my child's heart responded: "Here am I. Send me."

And God did—through college and seminary, into Christian ministry, into the world of writing, and into the most challenging faith walk of all: parenting. What a great adventure it all proved to be, fraught with pitfalls and punctuated with ecstasies. How I doubted myself, but God's indwelling presence was never in doubt. Always, if I could but wrangle a few moments of quiet solace, the peace of that divine connection would flood my soul with light and supply me with strength I did not own.

And then, without warning, night fell. While deep into the responsibilities of a demanding ministry position, at a time when I already felt inadequate and overwhelmed, God walked out. I remember the very moment when I realized it. I was offering communion at a women's retreat. I lifted the crusty loaf, broke it, and quoted Jesus' poignant and heartrending words: "This is my body, which was broken for you." At once, God's stabilizing presence — that indwelling strength that both warmed and bolstered me — expired like a tender flame in a storm. Standing before those beloved women, their faces upturned expectantly to mine, I felt stripped and horribly alone. Forsaken.

Somehow I trudged through the service, my words echoing round the empty walls of my soul. Then I fled to a private spot and wept. The night of God's seeming desertion continued for years, punctuated with blissful respites just when my hope gasped for its life. But for the most part, I suffered agony. Floundering beneath the icy waters of soul confusion, the surface was lost to me. My faith had become the breath-holding, teeth-gritting variety.

"Where," I begged God, "is my wrong? Show me the sin that has sent this icy deluge cascading over me." No response came, only the impression that I must wait. Tormented, I prayed harder, studied the Bible in a frenzy, flagellated myself for every real and imagined sin. Nothing helped. Nothing. Only a busy signal, only the necessity to wait.

All sweetness vanished from life; I begged God to take me home. Still the busy signal, still the icy sea. Each day proved unbearable, yet I had no choice but to bear it. Cursed beyond cursed I was, for God had forsaken me.

I learned, in time, to see it differently. When our pastor introduced a spiritual phenomenon called the dark night of the soul, my heart beat wildly in recognition. Then, in answer to one of God's mysterious commands (issued in a rare moment of communication), I entered the Episcopal seminary and came face to face with a tiny sixteenth-century monk named John of the Cross. Pouring through his short commentary *The Dark Night,* I found a kindred spirit. Five years into my night, John, with earnestness and compassion, explained its purpose. My night continued for over two more years, and though the agony of loss remained, my abject terror disappeared.

Were John of the Cross and I alone, then, in this dark misery? No. I suspect you, or someone you love, are enduring the night just now, a night that may last days, months, or sometimes years. The journey of the dark night is as old as humanity and will continue to be part of the faith walk as long as the world shall endure. How do I know? Travel with me to a skull-shaped hill on a day when darkness fills the afternoon sky.

—⟋⟋⟋—

A cry of consummate anguish tears through the man hanging on a Roman cross: *"Eli, Eli, lema sabachthani?"* "My God, my God, why have you forsaken me?"

Years before, a poet's tormented heart had poured forth the same words. Like the poet of old, Jesus experienced the desolation of God's turned back. Yet no one in human history has been so attuned to the Father, so devoted and obedient as Jesus. The Christ, already anguishing physically, suffered the terror of his Father's absence. Shall we conclude that Jesus was at fault? Shall we explain away his agony, saying Jesus merely quoted the Psalms to fulfill prophecy? Or shall we suggest that God cannot look on sin, and since Jesus became sin for our sake, God turned away?

But God does look at sin, long and hard. Every day. Indeed, God is determined to see us bring the broken fragments of our lives from behind our backs and look at them full on. Otherwise, how could God invite us to give our flaws into God's care so that, forgiven, we might rest in our Lord's loving embrace? Our God wills that nothing — no thing — come between God and us. Warts and all, we have God's love, hope, and attention.

Let us then hear Jesus' cry as an expression of solidarity with the human journey. Jesus chose to experience the heights and depths of our human life. He was tempted. Baptismal waters flowed over his body. He grew weary and hungry, suffered betrayal, and died. And Jesus chose to share our human experience by enduring the loss of God's comforting presence: the dark night of the soul.

But we hear conversations like these: "I don't feel God near me. I must not be disciplined enough in my prayer." "Perhaps I'm serving for the wrong reasons; God has turned away." "If God is distant, who moved?" Or we hear the same belief stated the other way around: "She feels so alone and she's such a good person. It's not right for God to make her suffer."

Is God's love attendant, then, on our behavior? Does God finally get fed up and walk out? In truth, God wants our company when we think and behave well — and when we do nothing of the kind. How do we know?

God is imaged often as our parent or shepherd. A parent who abandons a wayward child is the one at fault, not the son or daughter. God's unconditional commitment to us is infinitely greater than a mother's resolve to stand by the child she bore. And what shepherd throws up his hands when the sheep stray, declaring: "That's it. You guys are impossible. From here out, you're on your own." Instead, the shepherd calls each sheep by name — by name — and with the crook of his staff, he guides each wanderer back to the path. Such is the nature of love. And God is love.

So what if we've got it backward? What if the dark night is not some kind of punishment? What if God is not a cigar-chewing taskmaster? What if there is purpose in all this torment?

We are worth far more to God than what we accomplish or what we get right. The truth of that sentence, when it sinks in, can permeate and baptize the deepest, truest part of our soul. The rest follows naturally. God values us — period. No qualifications. God wants us, quite simply, out of love. The dark night is borne out of God's longing for you and for me.

So what if? What if the torture of the dark night has nothing to do with what we are or are not accomplishing and everything to do with how much God yearns to be in relationship with us? What if — just imagine it for a moment — what if God has walked away to entreat us to step closer and listen more deeply? What if God knows we are ready for deeper, more demanding relationship? What if the journey of the dark night is a blessing disguised as a curse? What if God has chosen to bless us?

What if… what if the dark night is sacred?

✠ *Why This Book?* ✠

I wrote *When God Walks Away* to be a compassionate companion in your dark night. This work cannot be called a self-help book, for the lesson of the night is that our help comes from God alone — even when what we have experienced as God has seemingly vanished. I hope you will consider this text a silent friend in holy mystery. *When God Walks Away* contains no solutions for the dark night. We cannot ward off the night as we would an insect attack. There is no repellant we can apply. Neither, if we are wise, would we so choose.

Rather, I hope this book serves as something you can tuck under your arm as you foray into the night's adventure: a reminder that you are not alone in your private agony. The book bears the names of God's faithful followers across time who have, like you, endured the night. Whatever wisdom resides between these covers reflects first the searching work of God, and then the testimonies of a great cloud of witnesses. I am grateful to include in that cloud those who consented to be interviewed for this work. I am deeply indebted to each one.

I have endeavored to use language that honors the fullness of God's nature. Therefore, while I use the pronoun *he* at one point, at another, I speak of God as mother. In this approach, I take my lead from Scripture and from the language of Jesus himself. I understand the overall revelation of Scripture to proclaim God as neither male nor female, but the fullest expression of both. I have written this text from the perspective of the Christian faith because I desire the book to honor Jesus, my dearest, most beloved companion. Moreover, Christianity was the faith of John of the Cross, who first used the term "dark night" to describe the experience of God's absence. However, I hope a person of any faith that honors relationship with God will find solace and challenge within these pages.

Sprinkled throughout the text are practices that helped me, or other dark night journeyers, survive the night by keeping an open line to God. At one point I'll suggest an art gallery trip, at another some musical expression, at still another journal writing as a way to bear the pain. Feel free to consider each practice as an item on a cafeteria line of nutritious selections. Some will suit your taste and some will not. Consider it a what-you-care-to-eat buffet — sample at will!

The dark night of the soul is a mystery as profound as God, its initiator. No amount of study could produce a writer equal to describing it. I feel rather like a blindfolded woman valiantly trying to describe an elephant by feeling only one of its legs. I can report in great detail what I know only in part! Therefore, in an effort at balance, the book includes the thoughts and imagery of souls across the centuries who participated in its mystery. We will welcome their guidance as we navigate the night's blind terrain. *Our journey begins in a brilliant darkness.*

INTRODUCING LIFELINES

Each section in this book closes with a "Lifeline," listing books, films, music, and artworks to accompany us and help us endure.

 Icon for books and literature

 Icon for film

 Icon for music

 Icon for fine art

Chapter Two

A Brilliant Darkness

I will lead the blind by a road they do not know, by paths they have not known I will guide them. I will turn the darkness before them into light, the rough places into level ground. These are the things I will do, and I will not forsake them. —Isaiah 42:16

We walk by faith, not by sight.
—2 Corinthians 5:7

His hair was white as snow in the sunshine; and gleaming white was his robe; the eyes under his deep brows were bright, piercing as the rays of the sun; power was in his hand. Between wonder, joy, and fear they stood and found no words to say.

—J. R. R. Tolkein, *The Two Towers*

For three hours we sat in the darkened theater as images of Tolkein's *The Two Towers* played across the screen and into our souls. The product of Peter Jackson's directorial genius, the movie — like the book — was dark: both visually and metaphorically. Stunned by the barrage of dark imagery, I stepped out of the theater and slammed my eyes shut, blinded. So strong was the afternoon sun's light against my eyes that, for a moment, all looked black. And then it hit me.

At the time I was deep into writing this book and seeking an image to encompass the dark night journey. God had just provided it. For here was John of the Cross's metaphor for the dark night — a light so brilliant it blinds.

God's light was not always blinding for me: in the beginning, God shone a tiny, tender stream into my childhood soul, leaving me warmed and comforted. Then, years later on the edge of the night, God turned up the beam a bit. I beheld vermin hidden for years in the dark recesses of my soul house. Sins that I'd believed long conquered were alive and quite well in me. God, in great compassion, had waited until I was strong enough to see the truth. Even so, it was almost too much. I could not run from the guilt; I could not work hard enough for God; my prayers sank like dust to my feet; the world turned a bleak gray. I had entered the first shade of night: the Night of the Senses. (The chapters "A Night of Surrender" and "A Sacred Suffering" explore the Night of the Senses adventure.)

Years into the night, after a season of reprieve, I received a blast of God's light that utterly blinded my soul. I grew convinced that God, disgusted with my weakness, had left me in the dark. In that hour, when God's absence seemed keenest, my soul actually bathed in divine glory. It was almost too much; in the night, God's light was darkness to my eyes. Despair was my dogged companion. This season of utter lostness and blindness was what John of the Cross called the Night of the Spirit. And it lasted for several years. (The chapter "A Relinquishing Death" probes the Night of the Spirit journey.)

The chapter "A Resurrection Surprise" describes life on the far side of the night. My eyes had adjusted to God's light a bit and I saw the world and myself in fresh, free, hopeful clarity. "Further Up and Further In," the book's final chapter, celebrates a homecoming yet to be: the eternal union toward which the Night draws each journeyer.

Great was the agony of that season and great is its gift. For in the night God took me on a journey into death, and at the dawn I was transformed and reborn. At the time I felt cursed and deserted; I now see the tender way in which God accompanied my suffering.

For throughout the dark journey, God brought to my waking mind and into my dreams scenes of Christ's suffering passion: a remembrance meal, prayer in a desolate garden, death on a cross, a silent tomb, and a surprising resurrection. Why? Looking back, I recognize God's loving intent: each event served as a signpost along the dark night highway. Each assured me that I was, indeed, headed somewhere: Jesus had gone before and therefore I could hope, somehow, to join him in a fresh beginning.

So one profound mystery informed another: as I accompanied Jesus' suffering, death, and resurrection, Jesus guided me safely through the night. And when the rigors of the night proved unbearable, when I lost the strength even to hope, I could look on Jesus in his suffering; I could hear his final words. And then I could not but love him. That love was my salvation in the night; without it I would not have endured.

In the night we, like Jesus, move through surrender into suffering and death. But the night delivers us into fresh, new, vibrant life. The resurrected Jesus was caught away into God's eternal now, and so shall we be one day. It is toward heaven, toward eternal union with our beloved, that the dark night draws us. Right now God's light blinds, but we have a constant, unerring guide: the suffering Jesus. Our guide's agony ended in joy beyond all imagining. And so, in time, shall ours. We will make our way through, but first we must begin. *The night's darkness is really blinding brilliance. But why must it hurt so much?*

PRAYERS IN THE DARK

Lord of Light, your brilliance has blinded my tender eyes. Take me by the hand and lead me. Amen.

Herein is my prayer — that I may see with your eyes what is to mine unseen. Amen.

LIFELINES

The Lord of the Rings by J. R. R. Tolkein: It's Tolkein — what can I say! I confess that I found the books wordy until I read them aloud to my daughter. Now I recommend reading Tolkein's trilogy aloud at least once (though not in one sitting!) for it washes our souls in its epic beauty.

The Lord of the Rings directed by Peter Jackson: Can anyone watch the *The Lord of the Rings* trilogy and doubt that film is art? Can we view these films without wondering to what impossible but vital quest God might commission us — and who would be our faithful Sam? And could we, Frodo-like, find ourselves one day transformed?

"Not by Sight" by Petra: It has enough rock drive to push me along my daily walks and enough confident faith to challenge me to endure, for one more minute, this darkness. The beat grounds me, and the words stick around for the day.

"Nights in White Satin" by the Moody Blues: Is this great stuff, or what? Lush with imagery of darkness and light, the smooth and the rough, this music feels like the mysterious night.

View of Toledo by El Greco: What could be more appropriate — a mystic, nocturnal portrait of the city in which John of the Cross endured his night, painted by a fellow Spaniard. El Greco's eerie, intriguing work suggests that anything could happen on this night in this place.

Chapter Three

A Night of Surrender

I am deeply grieved, even to death; remain here, and stay awake with me.
— Matthew 26:38

By his bruises we are healed.
— Isaiah 53:5

"I am sad and lonely. Lay your hands on my mane so that I can feel you are there and let us walk like that."

And so the girls...buried their cold hands in the beautiful sea of fur and stroked it and, so doing, walked with him.
— C. S. Lewis, *The Lion, the Witch, and the Wardrobe*

Father, if you are willing, remove this cup from me; yet, not my will but yours be done.
— Luke 22:42

I cast my eyes upon a kneeling man silhouetted against a sorrowing moon. His story and mine come together just now, in the midst of the night. He weeps salty, scarlet drops; agony shudders his furrowed brow. The lonely journey has begun. Those sleeping nearby are deserting even in their dreams. I hear the echo of words just spoken.

"Wait with me."

Amidst trees twisted like arthritic men, night deepens. I kneel beside him, my own body shaken with silent sobs. His body grieves in each heartbeat, and my heart moves to match his tempo. I see his brow bead in anguish, feel his faltering breaths.

Why am I here?

"Wait with me," comes the answering darkness.

If I am not willing to kneel beside my Lord in his anguish, how can I claim to love him? So I will myself to stay, to watch his struggle, to enter into and share his agony....

It continued that way for months. I couldn't get past the garden, couldn't understand why this image flashed into my waking mind and riddled my dreams. All I knew was God's call to remain, to wait through the night with Jesus.

It's not the sort of thing you tell your average friend.

"Hi! How's it going with you?"

"Well, I'm stuck in the Garden of Gethsemane."

No, I'd need to wait it out alone.

"Father, if there be a way, let this cup pass from me."

I kneel in the pregnant silence between question and decision, and live eternity between that utterance and the next. How keenly the tension of anguished hope gnaws me.

Can Jesus bear such brutal obedience? Does he not question such a hideous expression of God's love for humanity? Does he not recoil from the thought of torture, ridicule, and slow death? O God, there must still be another way.

There must be.

There must.

—But there isn't. This is it. God's only choice.

The form beside me moans; huddled shoulders lift. I hear an almost imperceptible sigh. Then the words come, quiet but ringing with resolve and filled with humble strength. Their sound on the night air chills my heart.

"Not my will but yours be done."

A circus of torch lights dances through the trees. Jesus' heart skips a beat — mine lurches to a stop. He stands, now resolute and ready, his choice fixed. With quiet assurance, Jesus walks through the indignities of trial and sentencing, betrayal and denial. I feel the sting of the whip and the stickiness of spittle. I hear him denigrated and mocked, questioned and condemned. But his abusers shame only themselves, for his eyes remember a baptism blessing: "You are my Son; my love and delight." Jesus knows — he always knows — who he is and to whom he belongs. Thus he can surrender. *But — can I?*

✠ *Why Me?* ✠

...the mystery of God will be fulfilled...
— Revelation 10:7

I happened on mystery books in the third grade: a girl three houses down had two shelves of tightly packed and yellow-backed Nancy Drews. She loaned me one, and I was hooked. After reading my way through Nancy's exploits, it was on to the Hardy Boys and the Bobsy Twins. *Emil the Detective* was, pardon the pun, a real find. Thanks to my seventh-grade English teacher, I met my all-time favorite detective, Sherlock Holmes. After I'd sleuthed my way through all of Conan Doyle's adventures, Agatha Christie's *The Mysterious Affair at Styles* beckoned from my high school library shelf, and I soon followed Poirot and Miss Marple through a host of mind-boggling cases. Bookstore shelves and PBS's *Mystery!* expanded my sleuth list: Perry Mason, Albert Campion, Cadfael, Lord Peter Wimsey. A mystery novel became my reward after surviving a rough final or, in time, a tough writing assignment. My husband is never at a loss when my birthday rolls around — I'm always up for a new whodunit.

What, I've often wondered, is my fascination with mysteries? Part of the attraction is sorting through clues, using a bit of intuition, then hitting upon the guilty party — and his motive — before the book's sleuth, leaning against the drawing room mantelpiece, reveals it to one and all. I'm drawn as well to the intriguing times and settings: a twelfth-century monastery in mythical Shrewsbury, turn of the century Baker Street, a courtroom in today's America. But, all in all, mysteries add up to something more intriguing than the sum of their parts: the "something" that gives the genre its name.

Ironically, this genre, that seeks by its final pages to tie up every loose end and round up each red herring, opens wide my imagination to those things that cannot be neatly knotted and classified. The writers, stirring up a murky mix of human passion, human reason, legalities, and moralities, invite me to look deep and wonder. The mysterious is, after all, that which baffles and eludes us. Thus, mysteries speak to my soul's yearning for the inexplicable, the expansive — those things I value because they won't be pinned down. Knowing there is so much beyond my knowing stretches me to grow wiser, to risk more often, to make of life an adventure.

Within each day's events, from the yielding of sleep to morning wakefulness through the melting of consciousness into healing sleep, lie God's mysteries. There is meaning beyond meaning, mystery beyond mystery, paradox within paradox, in each ordinary event. Yet for me, the dark and agonizing seasons form the greatest mysteries. What I cannot reason out, what my heart rages against, has the greatest potency for soul growth. Do I like these seasons? Not one bit. Do I want to live through them again? Not on your life. But I am grateful for what they invite me to become. And of all the mysteries of faith, the dark night is, for me, one of the most profound: it turns our prior assumptions on their ear and leaves us stricken and bereft — all in the name of God's blessing.

No string of clues will lead to the night's unmasking. No clever detective will emerge from the mist to tie up its loose ends. Yet the night is chock-full of mystery and adventure. We'll need to take off our shoes, for the very ground beneath us in this darkness is holy. *The night is a mystery — and a costly one. Will it not, perhaps, cost too much?*

WHY ME? PRAYERS

Lord of Mystery, in this dark place I know neither your presence nor your purpose. Are my questions any sort of answer? Amen.

You have wrested me from the sureties of my past. Give me the strength to live inside the mysteries of today. Amen.

LIFELINES

Strong Poison, Have His Carcase, Gaudy Night, and *Busman's Honeymoon* by Dorothy L. Sayers: Sayers took the mystery genre deeper when she introduced Harriet Vane to Lord Peter Wimsey; the fop finds his soul and with it, true suffering and a deeper life.

The Westing Game by Ellen Raskin: Raskin's Newberry Award winner is as intelligent and rascally a mystery as I've ever read — great stuff! Don't let the Newberry fool you — it's a great read at any age.

Mystery! Cadfael by PBS: Derek Jacobi is brilliant as the seasoned, centered monk of Shrewsbury Abbey (his tender care for the sick reminds me of John of the Cross!). Based on Ellis Peters's wonderful books, *Cadfael* looks on life's hardships with a sharply theological and keenly compassionate eye.

Gosford Park directed by Robert Altman: An English manor house, a party of the rich and famous, and an inexplicable murder — but this time it's those "below stairs" whom we need to watch. Despite one tasteless sexual encounter that doesn't fit the film's overall polish, it makes for a rollicking evening of viewing.

"Gethsemane" by Andrew Lloyd Webber: In Jesus' gutwrenching solo from *Jesus Christ, Superstar* resounds a rage, confusion, and weariness I know well. What Jesus felt in those moments is a mystery, but it is a mystery that calls my name.

"Stairway to Heaven" by Led Zeppelin: Bustles in hedgerows? No need to figure out the lyrics, just feel the yearning, invite the haunting melody in, and sing along.

Mona Lisa by da Vinci: Not only is this painting's conception and history mysterious, the piece itself whispers questions it refuses to answer. What is this woman feeling, thinking? Who is she, really? We look closely at her eyes, mouth, hands, and for an instant, seem to know. But then she changes somehow....

✠ *How Will I Now Live?* ✠

A stone was cut out, not by human hands, and it struck the statue on its feet of iron and clay and broke them in pieces. — Daniel 2:34

Drawn — even as a child — to mystery, I found the Bible's dream stories riveting. In one of my favorites, King Nebuchadnezzar expects his magicians to interpret a dream he cannot remember. If not, they'll all be killed. Such outrageous behavior from adults enthralls children. Young Daniel, depending on the God of Israel — the God I worshipped — does the impossible. He interprets the mysterious dream and saves the day.

But the dream itself, that was the real draw. The storyteller weaves a masterful tale, never revealing the nature of the dream until Daniel, the hero, speaks it aloud. At Daniel's words, my mind spun with bizarre images.

—⚒—

My childhood eyes gaze up at a statue — taller, far taller, than any building I've ever seen — carved in the fashion of the ancient Middle East. How it dazzles in the sun! How it captures my breath. It stands stern and solid, dwarfing all Babylon's inhabitants, Daniel included. The statue's head, cast in pure gold, reflects the noonday sun like a blinding beacon. Below it, a pure silver chest and two sterling arms flex proud muscles. The belly and thighs, cast of bronze, cannot compete with the dazzle of gold and silver, but they glow sturdy and solid. The legs of iron seem to my childhood eyes a bit rusted, but iron isn't known for beauty; it's the stuff of power. I lower my eyes to the feet, almost as tall as myself. I find there a muddled mixture of iron and clay: hardly feet worthy of that noble head and chest.

From a cliff nearby, an invisible hand hews off a rock and propels it with matchless precision toward the statue's feet. The great giant's foundations explode in clouds of dust. Then follows a chain reaction: the iron legs vaporize, then the bronze belly, the silver chest and arms, and last, the golden head. The wind catches up the once weighty mass and plays it out of sight. In the immense silence lay shards of broken clay. The hurtling rock grows and grows until it towers above me, cutting off the sun. Never have I seen a mountain so tall and strong.

—m—

When, a few years later, I heard the expression "feet of clay," I knew just what it meant. In the night, shining images I'd connected with God stood high above me, utterly indomitable. But when I looked down, each one had feet of clay. And God was aiming a rock at one after another. As each one shattered, a part of me quaked, too.

The night implodes our god images. No matter how much work we do for God, it never feels like enough; our spoken prayers seem to clatter, dead, at our feet; we lose all joy in God's good creation. What is happening to us? In truth, God is honoring us, taking from us images we have associated with God, so we might love God alone. But what a painful process that is!

Labor as God

It began healthily enough. As a young college student who had, for years, benefited from the dedication of Sunday School teachers, camp counselors, and ministers, I wanted to give something back. I truly loved teaching children's Sunday School and Vacation Bible School and writing devotional pieces. I'd found my life's vocation.

My ministry career began in a large church, working with hundreds of children and families: needs loomed everywhere. Ministers should be dedicated to show their love for Jesus, I decided. I must do all I can.

But no matter how hard I worked, I would read about someone who seemed more dedicated or I would hear a sermon or read a book entreating me to "give till it hurt" for Jesus. So I labored harder and longer, but I felt no sense of peace, no experience of God's pleasure. Instead, I focused on what I'd left undone or on where I had failed. Fatigue and illness were my constant nemeses, but I couldn't permit myself time off unless a doctor ordered it or I simply could not move from bed. How could I say no to Jesus?

I knew nothing of healthy balance between work, play, and rest. If I wasn't working, I felt like a sluggard. After all, if I really loved Jesus, I must show it by my labor. I was so resolute about going the extra mile that I went an extra twenty! But at self-care and boundary setting, I was quite hopeless. Even my daily quiet time stemmed from a sense of Christian duty without any notion that I might enjoy God's company and God might enjoy mine.

Truth is, though I never thought it out, that I lived as if labor for God equaled relationship with God. And the weight of impossible expectations — mine, not God's — quite nearly destroyed me. Indeed, God used the night to free me from my work-laden image. And I'm not alone in that.

A friend going through the dark night told me she had always associated church work with God. When night fell on her, she got busier — and she had been plenty busy before. The mysterious work of the night began when she suddenly lost her job and then became too ill to volunteer at church. When her work stopped, God got to work on her. She discovered the need for quiet and solitude. Now she does far fewer church tasks, but her time at church is richer and more worshipful.

My studies at the Episcopal seminary introduced me to a wise and humble monk named Benedict, who gave me a fresh perspective. Benedict created a "rule" for the monks in his monastery. His rule was, quite simply, a recipe for healthy living with equal portions of work, play, and rest. I had a hard time releasing my image of unceasing labor. Indeed, I still struggle with feelings of shame when I take time to simply be — but less and less often I'm relieved to say!

I needed to let my labor image topple because labor for God is not God and because work was tearing me apart. And with the relinquishment of my stern work ethic came an unexpected gift. The depression against which I'd battled since childhood eased, and, for the first time in my memory, I felt pure spontaneous delight. To God be the glory!

People as God

Because I've always felt like an oddball and an outsider, I've been drawn to people who appear to accept me or to understand some of my quirkiness. I would invest these people with the power to tell me whether or not I had worth. If they proved harsh or unfaithful, I suffered the worst agonies of shame. I bore every judgment and mistreatment as if it contained some hard but unfailing truth that I must accept and bear. Across the years I've subjected myself to some quite sizable portions of emotional abuse.

What then, was my problem? Simply this: I made gods of people, expecting them to always have my best interests in mind, giving their opinions more weight than my personal sense of truth, placing on them a weight no human can bear. But, like Nebuchadnezzar's statue, one after another, they crumbled before my eyes. Each time that happened, I tumbled headlong into confusion.

In the night I received some well-intentioned advice from people. But sometimes it just was not good advice. I remembered the story of a man who suffered a night of desperate agony: within months, he lost all his wealth; his children — every last one — died; he contracted a loathsome, debilitating illness; and his bitter wife taunted him to "curse God and die." Then, to add insult to injury, along came the friends who meant well. They sat in ashes with Job and gave him their take on the whole affair. They meant well; they just weren't right. And Job told them so. Finally, finally, I let go of my need to form people into God's image. How grateful I was for those few who came to sit with me in the ashes; their simple presence was gift enough.

People — God's people — are going to let us down. Why? Like you and me, they are creatures with creaturely limitations who err and sin and get up the next morning and give it another go. While struggling to relinquish the image of people as God, I crafted a life mission statement. It is, quite simply: *to love God and all creation; to serve God and all creation; to worship God alone.* The statement reminds me that it is fully appropriate to love and serve people. It reminds me as well not to confuse any creation — people included — with the Creator.

We all have feet of clay. But clay is good, earthy stuff. It's what we're made of, and it's exactly what we're meant to be. No more. No less.

Feelings as God

"But through it all I had God's peace in my soul."

I grew up hearing testimonies and sermons that promised God's peace through all of life's trials. Thus, I equated the promise of God's peace with a feeling of calm serenity. If I had enough faith, I believed, I'd be able to skate through each and every adversity wearing some kind of impenetrable peace gear. The spears and arrows of pain wouldn't even nick the fabric. Deep within, I'd always feel the bliss of God's presence.

Nothing prepared me for the battle that now ravaged my soul. If I believed enough in God, I screamed at myself, nothing would be able to really get at me. Yet I felt no calm, no serenity: only lostness and sorrow. What was I doing wrong? Was God punishing me? I couldn't muster the right God feelings.

The night had come to challenge beliefs that were holding me back. I believed the purpose of faith was to keep pain at arm's length. Yet I could never attain such a faith, for I am cursed and blessed with powerful emotions. Truth is, I was ashamed of the depth and breadth of my emotional experience. Mine has always been less a "peace gear" faith and more of the "wrestling in the darkness" sort. I was hiding from myself and from the world — especially in the season of darkness when I could not testify to God's peace or presence in my soul.

It was precisely the belief that I must *feel* God's presence that led me to conclude that God had walked out. But God had simply changed the form of our relationship, so I could grow up a bit.

The night taught me the difference between feelings associated with God and the reality of God's constant presence. A vast difference exists between feeling separated from God and being separated. Whether I feel good or not (I much prefer feeling good!), God is there. Feelings are statues with feet of clay; God is an eternal and solid rock.

Ideas as God

The dark night compelled me to question ideas I'd once thought equaled God (pre-night formula: ideas about God = God). In addition, classes at Austin's Episcopal seminary introduced me to theology unlike any I'd studied before. I'd drive home singing after one class because a new truth had thrilled me through, then a concept explored in the next class would so confuse my faith that I'd drive home in tears. How was I to know which ideas to affirm and which, if any, to toss?

God supplied an image that helped enormously. I imagined myself carrying an empty basket to class. As the professor offered a new idea, I placed it in the basket as a novel fruit or vegetable — possible sustenance for my soul. During class, I did not seek to analyze the concepts, merely to grasp them. Later, as I prayed, I imagined myself dumping the basket out on the ground before Jesus. One at a time, I would hold up a spiritual fruit or vegetable and ask, "Jesus what do you think of this? Is it good food for me?" If Jesus nodded, I put it in the basket to chew on. If not, I left it on the ground, realizing that as my soul matures, Jesus may invite me to later digest the edibles I'd set aside. Sometimes — quite often in fact — I received only silence in response to my question. At first

I panicked at Jesus' non-responses. In time I learned to entrust the ideas to Jesus and await his clear direction.

The dark night invites us to rest our questions in God. Honest doubt can till our soul ground, but regular times of contemplation are key. If we let our doubts endlessly churn at our soul's soil, nothing fresh can grow. We must take time to ask God, "What do you think of this?" One day new planting will begin. We can count on it.

Left to themselves, ideas are cold, harsh idols — as stern and unyielding as Nebuchadnezzar's statue. If the king's statue had proved more supple and yielding, the results might have been different (post-night formula: ideas about God can $\approx$ God). Ours is a living, breathing faith. A daily, growing faith. God invites us into relationship not with a doctrine, but with God — we must come heart first.

—m—

I stand and watch my past images of God, as tall and unyielding as Nebuchadnezzar's statue, teeter and plunge toward destruction. Each time, my heart quails at the loss — how will I now live? Yet with each implosion, I stand in the settling dust and breathe a prayer of thanks. These images were captors; they would chain me to the past. I stand in their debris freed to worship God alone. *We can learn to abandon much for God. But what about those who depend on us for spiritual nurture? Must we desert them as well?*

PRAYERS IN THE DUST OF TOPPLED IMAGES

God of my Labors: Work is my passion. Help me learn the holiness of rest. Amen.

Jesus, your friends deserted you. I know such desertion. Help me to trust that you have not fled me, too. Amen.

God of my feelings, I feel no sweetness, no peace of your presence. I ache with loss. Hold me, whether I can feel it or not. Amen.

God of my ideas: I rest my doubts in you. Make my mind as supple and eager as a growing tree. Amen.

LIFELINES

 Pride and Prejudice by Jane Austen: Who in this book did not have cause to rethink themselves? Austen, in her lighthearted but sharply satirical style, invites us to think again about what — and whom — we idolize. (The BBC miniseries starring Jennifer Ehle and Colin Firth is an excellent adaptation of Austen's book.)

Sabbath by Wayne Muller: A needful read for anyone (like me!) who equates work for God with love for God. Its short chapters and hands-on spiritual practices make a pragmatic as well as a thoughtful read.

A Christmas Carol by Charles Dickens: Hmmmm...what would you say Scrooge idolized? And if he were sent, Marley-style, to my chambers, what word would he have for me?

Footloose directed by Herbert Ross, *Chocolat* directed by Lasse Hallström, and *Babette's Feast* directed by Gabriel Axel: Each film begins with the expected — a status-quo churchology embodied in *Footloose*'s grieving pastor and father, in *Chocolat*'s repressive mayor, and, in *Babette's Feast*'s sisters who divinized their stern father. Ironically, the "pagans" in the films (Ren, Vianne and Babette) free the "professional Christians" to enjoy the Christ adventure.

"Things We Leave Behind" by Michael Card: What the mystics call detachment, Card describes through gospel stories.

Card's real-world theology calls it straight: it costs to let go, and freedom is worth any cost.

"Hi-De-Ho That Old Sweet Roll" by Blood, Sweat and Tears: Who can resist heaven described as "an old sweet roll"? The song explores the cost of living too much for the adoration of others and a freeing confrontation with the devil.

"Desperado" by the Eagles: Here's some old West, card playin' spirituality set to a tune that weeps. Is it a coincidence that desperado sounds so much like desperate?

Milo of Crotona by Pierre Puget: A mesmerizing, disturbing statue about a troubling, terrifying myth. Milo was so taken with his own strength that he tried to uproot a tree bare-handed, got his arm stuck, and was eaten alive by a lion. Let us hope our idols do not lead us to such desperate ends (bad pun intended!).

✠ *Must Night Fall on My Family?* ✠

I know that you fear God, since you have not withheld your son, your only son, from me.   —Genesis 22:12

One quiet Saturday afternoon our daughter Bethany — eighteen months old at the time — played under the kitchen table. Suddenly, her piercing screech split our eardrums, only to be followed by louder and wilder screams. We dragged her out and looked her over. Her tiny fist, clenched in a death grip, was swollen twice its normal size. As we pried open her fingers, a wasp flew out (albeit a little dizzily!). She had been stung multiple times because her instinct was to clutch when in pain. She had not yet learned that wasps do more damage when held tightly than when our hands are open.

—∿—

God brought this story to mind several years later as I prepared a sermon on a rich young ruler. Easily I connected a wasp's destructive power when clasped tightly with money clenched in our fist. But the story came rattling to consciousness again as I prepared this text. "Look again. Look deeper," God challenged.

One of the night's worst agonies was watching my children watch me suffer. Would my struggle cast a permanent shadow on my children's growing faith? I agonized over this question amidst the swirling darkness of God's night. At first, I expended massive energy to keep up appearances. I hid my tears behind closed doors and managed a stiff upper lip in front of my children. Yet they sensed my pain and suffered, too. Sometimes anger at God broke out in a snappish remark to my husband, David, or in harshness toward one of my daughters. Many times, enduring the night's rigors absorbed every ounce of my energy and attention. Of course, I didn't want to respond to my family so, and I steeled myself to do better next time round, but I failed — and I failed again. And it seemed God had failed — after all, if God were not tormenting me, I'd be a much nicer mom!

I wanted to give my children the best of myself; in the night, with its resultant depression, my best wasn't very good, at least to my mind. I felt a traitor to my own children, for we were all tumbling in the night.

But I wasn't betraying my children; I was merely staring at the hard fact of my own limits. In short, I had simply stumbled across my pride. True, I was not the mom I'd imagined I would be, but I was the only mom the girls had. And I would just have to get over myself.

So each morning, laying on my battered pillow, I prayed, "Here am I," and gave myself, empty and useless as I felt, into God's care. Then I would pray for my daughters, Arielle and

Bethany, asking God to use even my brokenness for their good. I wrote them letters, expressing my best hopes for their lives in Christ. And I said "I'm sorry" quite a lot. I'd begun to become real.

How did the girls survive my trip through the night? Arielle, my oldest, has walked through her own season of doubt and into a maturity of faith that awes me. She is the kind of person whom people go to when they're hurt, because she's not afraid of hard things.

My youngest, Bethany, at twelve, penned a poem that begins in struggling opposites.

> good and bad
> knowledge and the unknown
> joy and ridicule ...
> hope and doubt
> love and emptiness
> care and loneliness ...

She then explores the ultimate relinquishment:

> what is there after everything ends
> where do I go then
> where is there a perfect place
> where is the vast drop to death. . . .

And then she wonders with hope:

> maybe the things that we don't
> understand are the things that are
> better for us
> the good not the bad
> the knowledge and not the unknown

> joy not ridicule
> love without emptiness
> lots of care and no loneliness...
> the hope without any doubt.

I did not teach her such wisdom by being a perfect "spiritual soccer mom." God taught her on the rough road of life because she is, as is Arielle, God's own child. And I must trust God to care for God's own. *We cannot see where the night will take our children, so we entrust them to the only one who can. Is there, then, any human hand that we can clasp?*

LETTING GO PRAYERS

It's hard enough, Lord, to commit myself into your hands. Strengthen me that I might entrust to you those I hold most dear. Amen.

Lord God, heal my children from the wounds of my allegiance. Woo them as you did me until you become their love beyond all loves. Amen.

LIFELINES

Time Quartet by Madeleine L'Engle (anthology of *A Wrinkle in Time, A Wind in the Door, A Swiftly Tilting Planet,* and *Many Waters*): Though marketed as "family values" reading, there's more — much more — here. The heroes, including the supernatural ones, nestle into our souls; we grow to love them because somehow these people, these stories, are our people, our story.

The Lion, the Witch, and the Wardrobe and *Prince Caspian* by C. S. Lewis: Volumes one and four of the Narnia Chronicles, these books attest God's love for, trust in, and dependence on children. Who would not trust their beloved son or daughter to Aslan's care?

A River Runs through It directed by Robert Redford: This simply beautiful movie closes with a sermon for all who love someone.

Fiddler on the Roof directed by Norman Jewison: A jovial Job figure, Tevye is losing his children and his home. He takes it all in stride until one event rocks his faith. *Fiddler* is proof that musicals need not be fluff.

"Beautiful Boy" by John Lennon: "Life is just what happens to you when you're busy making other plans" — wise advise from father John Lennon to his son and good for us to remember in the night.

"Bring Him Home" from *Les Misérables:* When Colm Wilkinson sings "Bring Him Home" (the Broadway album), it's almost unbearable. His anguished prayer pleads with a desperation parents know well.

The Lost Sheep by Alfred Soord: Most Good Shepherd depictions look like someone who wouldn't last a day out of doors. But here is a determined, muscular shepherd with whom I can trust my lambs.

Migrant Mother by Dorothea Lange: Feel hopeless to protect your children? Lange's photo mirrors our anguish even as it tears out our hearts.

✠ *Is There Mending for Such Brokenness?* ✠

I have eagerly desired to eat this Passover with you before I suffer . . .
—Luke 22:15

The night of Christ's betrayal begins with an upper-room feast. Accompanied by the hollow clunk of pottery dishes stacked hurriedly for washing and surrounded by the pungent odors of roasting lamb, bitter herbs, and baking bread, a covey of men look to their leader. One follower wonders when Jesus will make his move: Passover is a perfect occasion for rallying the crowds against Rome. Another one fantasizes about his position in the new regime. A third congratulates himself for being the first to recognize their rabbi as the Messiah. One man fingers the silver coins in his hip purse.

Jesus motions them to silence, then looks each one dead in the eye and says with utter honesty: "I have eagerly desired to eat this Passover meal with you before I suffer."

—⁓—

I wrote earlier of the communion service when I first realized the night was upon me. It is with bittersweet emotion that I look back upon that mystery. It seemed at the time a brutal irony to lose my sense of God in the very service that commemorates Christ's presence among us. And something I alone knew turned that bitterness palpable. The single human communion in my life, intended to picture my relationship with Christ, had also broken. I'd all but given up on my marriage.

He was a most ardent suitor, returning time and again after my rebuffs (I had determined never to marry) and caring for me when a leg injury confined me to my apartment. When we spoke of books, of music, of beliefs, we completed each other's thoughts. Like David and Jonathan, our souls were knitted together. In time, God made it clear that this man was to be my husband. I grew to love David more deeply than any person in my life. And that's where the hurt began.

Not long after our wedding, David began to change. I could feel the walls going up around his soul; he shut his spirit away from me. All the vulnerability and openness of our courting days were gone. David, I discovered, has his own issues that made trust nearly impossible. And without trust, what hope had our marriage?

I had been tricked! Tricked by David, who promised me a loving, trusting relationship, but, most painful, tricked by God, who led me into the union. Had I not determined never to marry? Now I was married to someone who would share nothing of himself with me.

I tried everything to dismantle the wall around David's soul: I read books on marriage, prayed, went to — even hosted — marriage-enrichment seminars, talked, cried, yelled, dragged him to counseling, even threatened to walk out. Nothing. The fortress wall staunchly protected the pain within, pain at which I could only guess. And the fortress bricks could be dismantled only from the inside. After seventeen years and two children, I relinquished my hope for a marriage of spiritual intimacy. David met my disappointment with denial and bewilderment. To his mind, everything was fine. I was in this alone.

The marriage was as good as it was going to get, and I'd just have to accept it. But the sorrow of what could have been, the pain over what my children would not receive from their father, and the pressure of ministry was sinking me. Alone, I sought a Christian therapist; alone I made the agonizing decision to get on medication so I could function for my children and for my congregation. I had a brief respite until God ordered me — how stern God seemed at the time — out of my ministry position.

The greatest agonies of the night came several years after that communion service. By this time the ache within me was cavernous; I felt people could see the yawning hole where my soul should be. I yearned to sit in God's lap, to hear God promise: "I'm here. Everything's fine." But God had gone.

Most of my friends couldn't bear to see such raw suffering, and I stopped hearing from them. But — thanks be to God — the very agony borne of my lonely night began to work a miracle in David's soul. All things had worked together — shared soul night included — to mend David's battered soul from past injury. The wall crumbled, and the light within him shone with fresh brilliance.

Day after day, he told me to hang on to him. Night after night, he held me as I wept. Together, we prayed, sorrowed, and endured the night. A true sweetness grew between us in the very bleakest nocturnal hours. In the blackness of night, when I had no sense of God's presence, David was there. I could hold on to him, knowing God had given him to me. For years my marriage had seemed a burden. Now it was a lifeline. What I had despaired of ever having was mine — and immeasurably more. David, the hand to which I clung in the blackest of my night, knew — and knows — the worst of me and accepted me warts and all. Thanks be to God, who knows all!

———m———

And so we return to the night of Christ's betrayal. Sitting at table with the twelve, serving them his body and blood, Jesus knew their hearts. He knew Peter, all bluster and bragging, would deny him before Friday's dawn. He knew Judas had already spun a web of intrigue that would trap and kill them both. Yet he said, "I have eagerly desired to celebrate this meal with you." Jesus wanted these men with him. Did they understand what was in his mind? No. But they could, even with their limitations, accompany him. As a human, Jesus needed human touch. He asked them to wait in the garden, to keep vigil through the night. Not to leave him alone.

I, too, knew the desolation of aloneness. While the night's agonies were upon me, I spoke to few people; its intimacy and mystery drove me to silence. But, in addition to David, I did share with two women, both skilled in spiritual direction. Responding to my expressions of loneliness and confusion, one of them said simply, "I'd say I was sorry if I didn't know the result." Her discerning response fortified my parched soul with a taste of hope.

Who Hopes for Me?

If the title spiritual director is unfamiliar to you, your mind may conjure up the image of an ancient guru atop a snowy mountain. To those who make the climb and show due respect, he will reveal the meaning of the universe. In spiritual direction, however, the true director is the Holy Spirit. A spiritual director is someone whom God has gifted with the ability to welcome one and all without judgment, someone who will hope for us and challenge us spiritually, someone who can listen beneath the words with sensitivity, compassion, wisdom, and discernment.

Perhaps a friend, minister, or family member has served this need in the past, but when enduring the night, we do well to find someone trained in the subject. Spiritual directors meet regularly with directees — conversing, praying together, or sitting companionably in the silence of the Spirit.

Though more and more church staff ministers are receiving training in spiritual direction, Protestants may need to contact an Episcopal or Catholic church for a reference. There is no need to worry about theological differences. Spiritual directors are trained to respect other peoples' theological beliefs; their task is to listen, not to proselytize. If one director is not a helpful match, feel free to seek another. Appendix A lists some guidelines for selecting a spiritual director.

Can I Hope for Anyone?

I knew I needed some small community in the night, but what a surprise it was to find that others needed me as well. Even though I felt empty, confused, and directionless, people who hurt sought me out. Sensing a kindred spirit, they shared their stories. I understood their trust as an affirmation that my choice to be still was bearing fruit. And, as my pen scratched fury, confusion, and agony into my journal, images and themes emerged; I began to envision a book that would companion other journeyers through the night. Without the strange gift of the night, this text could not have been composed.

Although the night was intensely private, God cared for me, loved me, and encouraged me through a small and faithful community. And I had, even in my private torment, something to offer in return, born of surrender to the night. *The night guides us into a surprising, often unexpected, community. But even they don't know our journey. How can we tell where we're headed?*

PRAYERS IN BROKENNESS

For those who walk with me through the lonesome valley, Lord, I give you thanks. Amen.

I am too confused, too broken, too angry with you to help anyone, Lord. Help me help them anyway. Amen.

I am alone. No one knows my agony. The bread tastes stale and the wine bitter. Will I ever feel communion with you again? Amen.

LIFELINES

Who's Afraid of Virginia Woolf? by Edward Albee: Okay, this is *not* on my list of favorite light-reads. But George and Martha, in their bizarre, destructive relationship, are the ultimate marriage cautionary tale.

Two-Part Invention by Madeleine L'Engle: Marriage is seen as melody — not a falsely sweet tune, but one that plumbs disturbing depths while remaining true to the original composition. L'Engle ignores cultural marriage taboos and opens a window into her forty-year marriage from beginning to end.

A Beautiful Mind directed by Ron Howard: Promoted as the story of Nobel prizewinner John Naish, the film celebrates love's power. Amazing as Naish's determination and discipline is, his wife is the film's hero. Can love do the impossible? *A Beautiful Mind* says YES!

The Emperor's Club directed by Michael Hoffman: A quietly promoted and played film, I still think on *Emperor's Club* years after viewing it. As a teacher and minister, it blew me apart: have I set my sights on a select few, blind to the needs and gifts of others?

"Blackbird" by The Beatles: "Flying on broken wings" — who can live long in this world and not feel her heart rise at such words? Brokenness is its own beauty; less self-absorbed, more dependent on the grace of the wind, we fly freer.

The Glass of Absinthe by Degas: Ever felt more isolated in someone's company than if you'd truly been alone? In this moment, Degas' couple sits side by side in utter isolation.

The Dance by Henri Matisse: Painted in vibrant colors, this canvas celebrates both individual — male and female, the stumbling and the graceful, the energetic and the lithe — and community. All clasp hands in a living, dancing circle.

✚ *Am I Lost?* ✚

. . . this is God, our God for ever and ever. He will be our guide forever.
— Psalm 48:14

When, as a child, I embarked on my Christian journey, I toted along a divine road map that I trusted would guide me safely to my destination. It contained quotes from parents, pastors, and Sunday School teachers, my understanding of certain scriptures, and the doctrines of my Baptist heritage. For years, the map's images served me well, guiding me through some pretty tough terrain. But after a while the map ran out. That tiny roadway I trudged along ran straight off the top. Now I stood at a crossroad with no notion of which path to take.

Panicked, I scrutinized both the map and myself; surely I had missed something or made some fatal error. But try as I might, the illustration offered no more; the cartographer had not sketched this part of my journey. The map's tiny lines and letters floated before my eyes, while a terrified thought formed in my mind: maybe the whole trip was nothing but a wild goose chase. My head told me any good map should take me precisely where I needed to go. The tool I'd relied on had not only failed, it had landed me in danger and confusion. I was lost in foreign terrain. The sun set with terrible finality, and a chilling wind bit through my clothes.

I stood at the crossroads, probing the map for answers it could not yield. Then came the temptation: I could fall in love with the map itself. I knew it well already. I could grow to delight in its texture, the fineness of the cartographer's line, how comfortably it fit what I wanted to believe. I could stop here, set up camp, and get comfortable. In time, the map could become my destination, and I would live bewitched at the crossroads, the journey long forgotten.

So what would it be: familiarity and comfort — or faithfulness and fear? Something in me would not settle down or settle for less. Alone and deserted, I stood, trembling, in the dark night.

—ɯ—

Looking around at the crossroad, I discovered two other bewildered journeyers just as lost and despairing as me. They thought they understood God's plans; they believed they were on the right track. Then their maps ran out.

Here, on a dusty road between Jerusalem and Emmaus, we catch a God's-eye glimpse of the dark night journey. Two travelers shuffle along, deep in a dark night. They'd believed that Jesus was a prophet — the prophet — but Jesus is no more. They thought he would save Israel, but what use is a dead rescuer? Everything they believed in, everything they'd relied on, lay smashed.

Yet disguised to their wounded eyes, God walks alongside them that first Easter Sunday, listening with interest — perhaps even with a bit of merriment — to their conversation. I like to imagine Jesus at this juncture with a twinkle in his eyes. When Jesus asks why the two journeyers are so glum, they describe their sense of his failed mission.

Jesus listens to their sorrow, and then he explains "all the Scriptures concerning himself" (Luke 24:27 NIV). What a Sunday School lesson that must have been! Enraptured, the pilgrims find themselves compelled not only by the man's words, but also by the man. What is it about him? When they press him to stay over, the stranger agrees. In this they do well, for God appears in strange garb during the night.

Jesus takes bread, blesses it — and they know him. Does he resemble the person they had called Messiah? No — and … yes! In a new way: different, yet, in the heart of things, just the same. That's why they felt drawn to him. That's why their hearts burned.

—⁓—

We have maps because we need them. They point us in the right direction, but they can't take us there. At the same time, if we don't look at our map, we'll never set foot on the road. In the dark night we are between maps.

As I stood, shivering at that crossroad, people asked, "What are you up to now?" What could I say? That I was waiting for a new map? Yet waiting was precisely the work to which I was called. So I stood, sometimes patiently, ofttimes not, until I took in the map's message as a living teacher. I remained stranded until I discovered a new map tucked in my back pocket, one I was just then ready to decipher. Thanks to my crossroads time, I better grasped this map's potentials — and its limitations.

My God maps could point in the right direction, but they were, after all, only pictures. God alone deserves the whole of my allegiance. I said a hearty thanks to the old map, studied the new one with rising excitement, and stepped forward into a new adventure.

Mapless Prayers

I'm lost, Jesus. I'll stand still and wait for you to find me. Amen.

Give me courage, Lord, to look beyond the comforts of my past beliefs to your next great adventure. Amen.

LIFELINES

Catcher in the Rye by J. D. Salinger: Yes, the language is horrific. Yes, I feel deranged by the time I finish reading it. And, yes, I think it's a story too amazing to miss. Who in this story is mapless? Who provides directions?

Gone with the Wind by Margaret Mitchell: The Old South found itself, almost overnight, mapless. Where did that dark journey take their souls?

The Point directed by Fred Wolf: Harry Nilsson wrote it, and it's worth a watch for that. Oblio, a castaway misfit, has lost everything but his trusty dog, Arrow. Some quirky characters lead him to an unexpected point.

Valley of the Dolls directed by Mark Robson: Okay, so it's trashy. But when Neely screams in that alley, she's the picture of maplessness.

"Boulevard of Broken Dreams" by Green Day: In both lyrics and melody, "Boulevard" declares a loneliness and longing, a hopeless hope, that calls to us in the night.

The Supper at Emmaus by Caravaggio: The chapter "A Relinquishing Death" describes this piece in depth. For now, let's think of it, and the story that precedes it, as the dark night from God's perspective.

✠ *Toward the Cross* ✠

At long last, I walked with Jesus from the garden and deeper into the night. I shuddered against what I new was next to come.

Prayers of Submission

I've a strong will, God, which you gave me. I'm not sure I'm capable of submitting even to you, but help me try. Amen.

Father, if you are willing, take this cup from me; yet not my will, but yours be done. Amen.

Chapter Four

A Sacred Suffering

He was despised and rejected by others; a man of suffering and acquainted with infirmity.
—Isaiah 53:3

Yet it was the will of the LORD to crush him with pain.
—Isaiah 53:10

He poured out himself to death.
—Isaiah 53:12

I was alone, forgotten, without escape upon the hard horn of the world.
—J. R. R. Tolkein, *The Two Towers*

Meanwhile, where is God?
—C. S. Lewis, *A Grief Observed*

Surely he has borne our infirmities and carried our diseases....
—Isaiah 53:4

Amid the dead, dry jeers of the crowd and the hollow clank of Roman armor, we arrive.

Not this hill, Lord. Not this scene.

If I must look, I want to gaze up at him from below as one of the crowd. I'll even wear the label of one who shouts "Crucify him!" only let me distance myself from his suffering. But God lifts me up until I hang eye to eye with him — myself a thief suspended on a neighboring cross.

My Lord's chest shudders with the agony of breath; a sluggish breeze stirs a tangle of hair not yet matted to his brow. Fresh rivulets of red pour from new wounds in his wrists. I smell the stench of cheap wine and the salt odor of dying sweat.

O God, I cannot bear it — how can I endure the sight of your suffering?

"Do you love me?" Jesus' eyes implore.

"Jesus, you know I love you."

"Then stay."

Is this, then, the price of love? I know instantly that it is.

—⟋⟍—

I have two dear friends — a minister of great integrity and his spunky wife — who have suffered at the hands of not one but two churches. I was privileged to be there for them during part of their hard journey.

"Call me anytime," I said. We suffered through it together.

Then I faced a time of deep and private suffering.

"Call us anytime," they said. And I did. For months on end, they listened as I wept into the phone. I sat in their home and poured out my pain: "Why did God let this happen?"

I didn't need them to supply an answer, only to be a safe place where I could to pose the question. Without them to accompany my suffering, I don't know what I would have done. Their willingness to wait a while with me, to let suffering do its work without rushing it along for their comfort, to minister to my need without the praise or even the knowledge of others, was integral to my healing.

—〰—

And so I gaze on the bloodied face and broken body of my Lord, remembering the many times he befriended my agonies. The sky darkens against the atrocity of his suffering. Each cell of his dying body feels the iciness of the Father's absence; I feel it, too.

His cry, ragged with loneliness and grief, rings through the blackness: *"Eli, Eli, lema sabachthani?"*

✠ *Has the World Gone Mad?* ✠

When Jesus had received the wine, he said, "It is finished." Then he bowed his head and gave up his spirit. — John 19:30

I stand now beside a woman who, with stricken but unblinking eyes, beholds the slow, insistent suffering of her Lord's body. What events brought her to this place? Why is she here? What is he to her? What is she to me? How do our stories connect beneath this cross?

—〰—

They hammered in my head day and night, year upon year, until I did not know waking from nightmare. They screamed at me to destroy myself and gnawed me until I tore at my hair to rid myself of their teeth.

Then, in a flash of rational thought, I'd know the demons had me, that they played sordid games with my mind, and that I could not stop them. Those rare moments of sanity were nearly as bad as the demon times, so enraged did I become at my powerlessness against my attackers. A fit was on me when I first heard his voice; like soothing balm, it bathed my ravaged mind.

He laid calm hands upon my matted, sweaty hair. Again I heard his voice and looked up into his eyes. I read in them sorrow; I'd seen that look and knew what would follow, what always followed — first the shock of horror and then the embarrassed dismissal.

Not so this time. His eyes sharpened and focused, a piercing power. I was now the fearful one, the one who wanted to turn away.

"If I let him, he may heal me; but if I yield, I could die."

"Then die," I told myself. "For what life is this?"

I relaxed my will against his ministrations. A screaming began — one voice, then another, another, another....

Was I screaming? I never knew.

I woke to a reasoning mind. For the first time, my eyes looked on a world both sharp and clear. For the first time, I knew who I was, free of the voices that ate at my mind. So I followed the one who gave me life; I listened to his wisdom, watched him heal others, served as I could. Though Peter first named him the Christ, I had known from the beginning the kingly potency of his eyes and voice. He had come for some great purpose, that I knew. I could not wait to see his power unleashed against the Romans as it had been against the demons of my mind.

But now he is arrested. Tried. Sentenced. Crucified. He is gone, forever gone. Tomorrow is beyond bearing; I live for today alone. I remain with him in this hour though my heart aches with grief. My presence is a small gift, for I can change nothing. I cannot rescue him from his tormenters as he delivered me from mine.

I lift my eyes to the cross, its bulk creaking wildly in the wind. I can barely see his face, disfigured by blood, sweat, and pain. Life *pours down the naked wood, pooling red at its base. I bear the horror of it only out of a love that takes me past myself.*

The sky goes black; he screams against the darkness. Terror sends my heart racing. What now? Will the world — will my world — return to madness? Yes, for we are surely mad already. We are killing my Lord.

In the darkness, his voice rings with wild power: "It is finished!" He is dead.

I stand there, forgotten, as they disentangle his limbs from the nails, as they wrap his body and bear it away. Far behind the sorrowing procession, I follow, lost in solitary grief. At Sabbath's end I will come to his tomb — a final tribute — and do what I can. It will not be enough. But in a world gone mad, it will be, at least, something.

                                        —Based on Luke 8:1–2

—⟐—

For me, too, Mary.

Standing in the night beneath the cross, I, like my companion Mary Magdalene, had no sense of tomorrow. My world, too, had gone dark and spun into madness. I had only the knowledge that Jesus was everything to me, that I must wait in suffering. So I put my arm across her shoulder, and together we wept.

—⟐—

On Good Friday we join Mary Magdalene, bearing the agonies love demands. On Good Friday we look with tortured eyes on a world gone mad. On Good Friday we suffer the question "Why?"

> Why did my Lord die? Or my spouse...or my parent...or my child?

> Why did my parents abuse me?

Why am I estranged from my son?

Why did God let this happen?

My God, my God, why have you forsaken me?

Some suffering is beyond comprehension; rational answers cannot satisfy our aching questions. Astonished sorrow weights our hearts as we recall the 2004 tsunami that killed hundreds of thousands and ravaged entire nations. September 11, 2001, was and is an atrocity. Period.

Some atrocities come to our door. One Christmas season a few years back, my cousin walked past an array of twinkling, cheery holiday lights and into her mother's house. There she discovered the tortured, murdered bodies of her mother and niece. My cousin will endure that memory for the rest of her life. My mother has suffered through not one, not two, but three criminal trials, reliving her sister's death time and again. Another atrocity. Incomprehensible.

Jesus supplied no easy answers to hard questions, but he lived, suffered, and died among us. When my heart aches with suffering and my mind forms no answers, I close my eyes and see Jesus hanging on a cross, suffering alongside me. I am — you are — not alone.

Good Friday frees us from the need to fire off ready answers or dish out platitudes. It strengthens us to accompany those who suffer, to be a steady hand to which they can cling, to offer prayers forged in the crucible of our own heartache. Our tears mingled with theirs have healing power. *In the night, we learn the cost of love. But is it just one-sided devotion? Where, after all, is God?*

PRAYERS FOR SANITY

The world, my world, is mad with loss and rage and sorrow. Don't give up on us, Lord. Amen.

We are small and lost and hurt, Lord, but we love you as we can. Amen.

LIFELINES

The Singer by Calvin Miller: The strongest in a trilogy of poems (fear not, they're readable poems), Miller sings anew an old, old story, and we feel its violence and pathos afresh.

The Passion of the Christ directed by Mel Gibson: It begins in agony and does not let up until literally the film's last seconds. Excruciating — almost impossible — to watch, *The Passion* is also beautiful and epic-sized. Flowing through its murderous madness run two clear streams of sanity: Jesus' commitment to his call and Mary's love for her suffering son.

"When I Survey" by Isaac Watts and Lowell Mason: I'm nuts about hymns — poetry, living theology, compelling music; let's not lose such majesty. "When I Survey" weeps with the madness of divine love.

"Question" by the Moody Blues: Why can we never get answers to our hardest questions? The Blues ask theirs right out loud.

Guernica by Picasso: Depicting the bombing slaughter of a small Basque village in northern Spain, Picasso's riveting work screams against the insanity of all violence.

The Magdalen in Penitence by Donatello: Donatello, near the end of his life, depicts Mary near the close of hers. She bears the scars of hard living, but she wears the face of faith.

✠ *Am I Abandoned?* ✠

Why, O LORD, do you stand far off?
Why do you hide yourself in times of trouble?
— Psalm 10:1

My immediate sense of the night was that I'd been securely
locked out. I stood on tiptoe, palms against an icy stone edifice,
peering through a window into a room I'd once called my own.
God and I had dwelt there together from my childhood. That
space had been always the safe haven to which I could return
when life's storms battered me toward breaking. I'd expected the
cozy furniture and warming fire would always be mine.

Now, shivering in the wild wind, even the room seemed al-
tered. Cold shadows enveloped the furniture, and the fireplace
yawned dark and empty before my terrified eyes.

And what had become of God, my constant and comforting
friend? If that shadow in the corner was God — I couldn't be
sure — it was only God's cold, turned back. No battering from
the outside elements froze me as did that image.

I hammered on the door, turned the knob, and threw my
weight against its bulk. But I had a growing sense that, though it
had opened easily enough in the past, the entrance had been forever closed to me. The house — my soul house — was sealed tight.
I was at the mercy of the shadowy form with its turned back.

If, indeed, there'd ever been such a companion. What if I'd
imagined it all? What if I'd been, for years, the butt of some incredible cosmic joke? Beneath me the earth shook and reeled.
Did I dare ask such questions? Did I dare put my faith to such
a test?

As it stood, I had two options. I could tarry in the snow, stare
through a cold window, and imagine myself inside, in hopes that

pretence could will the past into the present. I could stand there for years, watching dust gather on the windowsill, straining my eyes for a glimpse of a shadowed back, feeling my bones grow old. But, frankly, the room, seen from the outside, looked stern and rather foreboding.

Or I could turn around, face away from the cold security of my past, and step forward into whatever I might find. The world outside my soul house didn't look too inviting either; cold, sterile, and threatening seemed more appropriate descriptors.

There I stood like Seuss's Grinch with my feet "ice cold in the snow." And every bit as puzzled. It was a solitary business, for the choice was mine alone to make. Yet, perhaps not so solitary. As I searched around for a guide — someone who had also suffered God's desertion — I found, to my surprise, my favorite writer.

Lewis's Forthright Grief

C. S. Lewis, a deceptively ordinary-looking man, was born in Belfast, Ireland, in 1898, the younger of two sons. He survived a perplexing, grief stricken, and sometimes harrowing childhood. By the time he'd become a professor at Oxford, Lewis had found his way out of, and then back into, the Christian faith. He titled his conversion autobiography *Surprised by Joy,* but there was yet another joy — a woman named Joy — to enter Lewis's life.

Their relationship began in lively cross-continental correspondence. Later, after leaving her abusive husband, Joy Davidman settled in England. In a civil ceremony Lewis married her, thus securing her English residency; it was a marriage in name only.

Unknown to either, advanced cancer had already chewed away much of Joy's thighbone. The doctors gave her very little time. Realizing his love for Joy and the prospect of her death, a stunned Lewis arranged a Christian wedding ceremony in her hospital room. Then a miracle occurred—Joy went into remission! During their brief wedded years, Lewis's heart knitted with Joy's. However, the cancer returned, and four short years after their wedding, Joy died. Lewis was lost. It seemed to him that when Joy died, God turned away as well. In journals lying around the house, he recorded his dark journey through grief.

I happened upon Lewis's journals, published as the small book *A Grief Observed*, long after my introduction to his works. I'd received a set of the *Chronicles of Narnia* as a college graduation gift and, as a young seminary student, would sit outside my apartment, open a volume, and lose myself in Narnia. I was drawn to Lewis's childlike wistfulness, to his wisdom, and to his open heart. Soon I was reading everything Lewis I could get my hands on.

When I drew a Lewis book from my shelf and nestled into the sofa, I felt him sitting at my side: a wise and compassionate uncle taking great pains to help me see what he was onto. Most of his books are written with a gentle chuckle throughout by the sort of man who could one moment imagine a faun carrying an umbrella in the snow and the next envision a demon counseling his inept nephew on the art of temptation.

But *A Grief Observed* accompanied my night most profoundly because of its starkness and raw pain. Reading it was like being dumped in a tub of ice water when I'd expected a warm bath. But ice water was the proper tonic for Lewis's subject, and I respected his courage and forthrightness.

Four words from *A Grief Observed* rang in my aching soul: "Meanwhile, where is God?" I found the line within the following quote: "Meanwhile, where is God? . . . go to Him when your need is desperate, when all other help is vain, and what do you find? A door slammed in your face, and a sound of bolting and double bolting on the inside. After that, silence. You may as well turn away. The longer you wait, the more emphatic the silence will become. There are no lights in the windows. It might be an empty house. Was it ever inhabited? It seemed so once."

Yes! The vacant house! Lewis had been locked out as well. The quote continued: "I tried to put some of these thoughts to C. this afternoon. He reminded me that the same thing seems to have happened to Christ: 'Why hast thou forsaken me?' I know. Does that make it easier to understand?[1]"

Jesus locked out? Forsaken? What kind of reckless love drove him to that cross of isolation? As I poured again through the book, I struggled with Lewis through confusion and grief. Midway, I felt a turning. "On the other hand, 'Knock and it shall be opened.' But does knocking mean hammering and kicking the door like a maniac?"[2]

On the book's final pages I read with ravaged hope these words: "When I lay these questions before God I get no answer. But a rather special sort of 'No answer.' It is not the locked door. It is more like a silent, certainly not uncompassionate, gaze. As though He shook His head not in refusal but waiving the question. Like, 'Peace, child; you don't understand.' "[3]

I didn't understand either: why should Lewis feel locked out when he ached for God's assurance? Why should Jesus feel forsaken? Why was I, in some fashion, sharing their anguish?

Parzival's Solitary Quest

Lewis's writing had not provided me with any answers, but it did accompany my questions. I began finding allusions to God's turned back throughout literature. One day my daughter Arielle returned from the library bearing a copy of the legend *Parzival* as retold by Katherine Paterson.

"I knew you liked her writing," Arielle explained.

Such is the mystery of God's teaching love. Here was as wise and witty a piece of writing, as true and probing a tale of the Christian journey, as I had ever read. My brief summary is a mere shadow of the story.

By choosing courtly legalism over compassion, the young knight Parzival failed his uncle, the Grail King, and exiled himself to a despairing, solitary quest: he must find the Grail Castle and right his wrong. Deep into his bleak journey, Parzival succumbed to despair; he concluded that God was set against him.

One wintry night Parzival stumbled into a hermit's cave, where, warmed by a fire and by human acceptance, the beaten knight unloaded his burden. "I vowed to serve one called God, but he is the grandfather of all my troubles."[4]

Reminding Parzival of Christ's suffering on the cross, the hermit encouraged the knight to trust God's companionship and renew his quest. Parzival soon "happened" on the mountain of the Grail King where the suffering monarch lay in his chambers, the agony on his face like the countenance of one who suffered on a cross. "Tears sprang to Parzival's eyes and he cried out, running as fast as his heavy armor would allow. He fell on his knees beside the king. 'Dear Uncle,' he said, through his sobs, 'what is wrong with you?'

" 'God be praised,' the king said. 'You have come at last.' "[5]

I knew too well Parzival's solitary journey. The world outside my soul house felt like bitterest winter. I, too, felt betrayed, directionless, and deserted. God was the grandfather of all *my* troubles. I knew with Parzival the desperate need to give up on God, and I tasted the desperate hope that compelled me to hold fast this one more minute.

Locked out like Lewis.

Betrayed like Parzival.

Forsaken like Jesus.

Yet each one moved through darkness and suffering: Lewis wrote his journal, Parzival mounted his horse, and Jesus, the greatest risk taker of all, yielded his spirit to an absent Father.

Heartened, I took a wavering step away from the security of yesterday's soul house and into the terrifying world of present reality. I had never felt so lonely or so terrified. But the stinging cold began to waken me as if from a very long sleep. A red cardinal on a snowy branch sang of God's majesty. Snowflakes melting on my sleeve proclaimed God's artistry. I stumbled, and a stranger helped me to my feet. My own breath, made visible by the cold, confirmed that, though I felt dead and deserted, I did, indeed, live. And that with life came new possibility. *Today's faith is cold and foreboding, but it's all we have. Is it even worth trying anymore?*

Vacant House Prayers

Oh, God, do be faithful. You seem to have deserted me, gone AWOL. It seems no future opens before me, rather that I am standing in the deepest of fogs, lost and terribly alone. Amen.

Where are you, God? You've disappeared somehow, and I fear the future without you. Help me believe that the courage I find to go forward into the cold comes from the warmth of your great love. Amen.

LIFELINES

Parzival (or *Parsival*) by Wolfram von Eschenbach: Von Eschenbach committed the legend to paper, and Katherine Paterson translated the story into a children's book. Eschenbach's story is linguistically rich; Paterson's is clean and clear. Both tell a witty, wise story of stumbling faith.

A Grief Observed by C. S. Lewis: A painful, though quick read that leaves a deep, clear impression.

Psalm 137: Can Scripture shock? Read the entire psalm from its weeping abandonment to the desires of its rage.

Shadowlands directed by Richard Attenborough: Based on the book *Through the Shadowlands* about Lewis's and David-man's lives, the film explores loss — of life, of faith, of childhood fantasy. As Lewis, Hopkins's eyes speak an unbearable pain. Even so, the film is a hopeful, magical piece of work.

A Man for All Seasons directed by Fred Zinnemann: Sir Thomas More knew abandonment. Everyone, including and especially his church and king, either deserted him or tried to force him to desert himself.

"Sometimes I Feel Like a Motherless Child" arranged by Harry Thacker Burleigh: Spirituals don't sugarcoat life. Poignant in melody and lyrics, this song names my experience in the night. Yet it ends in determination: "Sometimes I feel like an eagle in the air." Perhaps we're headed somewhere, after all.

The Wanderer in the Mist by Caspar David Friedrich. Wow! What a strange, isolated, entrancing work this is! I feel cold just looking at it, but I cannot turn away. There's something here that calls to me.

✠ *Why Even Bother?* ✠

. . . he went to the synagogue on the Sabbath day, as was his custom.

—Luke 4:16

My Baptist upbringing instilled in me a regular practice of Bible reading and prayer for which I'm most grateful. Most of the time I view the discipline as a gift I give myself rather than as an arduous chore to check off my To Do list.

In daylight hours, I looked forward to my quiet time when I visited with my dearest friend. The season of quiet prayer and Bible study nourished my soul like a tasty multivitamin. But in the night, such disciplines tasted like a foul tonic on my soul palate. It was a chore to do them, for I was angry and wanted to give God the silent treatment. Worse yet, the prayer walks that had highlighted and delighted my daylight times became torture. I was beset with the worst kinds of thoughts — rage against those who had wronged me, despair over my life's situation, and jealousy toward people who seemed to have an easier, pleasanter life. Guilt and self-loathing added their own bad tastes. All in all, I'd much rather have lost myself in a mindless novel or TV sitcom.

Knowing that John of the Cross had suffered similar agonies in a Toledo prison without any source of distraction challenged me. Knowing that John came through his dark torture and then wrote of it with simple joy and gratitude gave me comfort.

So in the night I made myself pray. I made myself open the Scriptures and then open myself *to* the scriptures. I brought along my anger and feelings of abandonment. And why not? God knew exactly how I felt. In those alone hours, I scratched rage onto page after page of my journal, imprinting it in large, violent letters. Sometimes I shouted my protests aloud in the empty air.

I hoped to feel healed after these practices — freed of my anger and lifted from the dark-night shroud. It didn't happen that way. Yes, sometimes a phrase of Scripture gave me strength and insight to accompany my day. Sometimes I could feel the cleansing power of prayer. But only sometimes. I came to realize that my feelings weren't the point.

Spiritual practices, whether they tasted foul or delicious, expressed my love and faith. In doing them I said, "I don't feel you, God, but I believe you are there, and I am willing myself to be here." Making myself available to God was the needful thing. Feelings were an accompaniment to the real purpose of spiritual practice: showing up.

I often grew weary and resentful of the practices. Cod liver oil may be good medicine, but I never knew anyone eager to swallow a dose. When I got thoroughly disgusted, I'd remember Aslan's signs.

Remembering the Signs

In the Narnia Chronicle *The Silver Chair,* the great lion Aslan commissions Jill and her companions to a rescue mission. To Jill alone, Aslan commits four signs and a warning: "But, first, remember, remember, remember the signs. Say them to yourself when you wake in the morning and when you lie down at night, and when you wake in the middle of the night. And whatever strange things may happen to you, let nothing turn your mind from following the signs. And secondly, I give you a warning...as you drop down into Narnia, the air will thicken...the signs which you have learned here will not look at all as you expect them to look, when you meet them there. That is why it is so important to know them by heart and pay no attention to appearances. Remember the signs and believe the signs. Nothing else matters."[6]

Due to peevishness or willfulness or forgetfulness, Jill and her companions muffed the signs many times over. Of course, she got tired and forgot to recite them nightly, but each time Jill remembered and tried again, the mission got back on track. In the end, the travelers rescued the prince and received Aslan's praise.

In the night, I likened Aslan's signs to God's truths and the task of reciting them to spiritual practice. I felt heartened that Aslan did not give up on the children when they failed in their practice. Like Jill, the moment I returned to a neglected practice, God began with me where we'd left off. I needed all the grace I could get, and God was good to give it.

What, then, is a spiritual practice? Quite simply, it is any discipline that keeps us connected with God. A discipline of regular spiritual practice is needful in the night, but it does taste, at times, like cod liver oil. So why take a daily dose? In fact, why bother at all?

Because We Need Connection

In my early Christian life, my motive for spiritual practice grew from teachings that these were things that good Christians do. But at the end of the day, I'd look back with guilt because surely I could have done more. I could never be a good enough Christian, could never feel at peace with myself.

The night taught me the point of spiritual practice: connection with and awareness of God. Spiritual practices express my love for God, they answer "yes" to God's loving invitation: "Come aside a while; stay with me." What parent would not delight in any demonstration of affection from a beloved child? When my daughter appears with a fistful of wildflowers gleaned from our backyard, I don't say, "Why didn't you bring me flowers yesterday, or the day before?" I don't bark, "There are only seven flowers here. I demand eight!"

Because We Need to Endure

In Tolkein's *The Return of the King,* Frodo toils toward Mount Doom, where he must fling the ring of power into the fires that forged it. It's an impossible assignment. Already he has journeyed too long and endured too much; all hope has left him. Frodo expects to die before completing his mission, but on he toils though wounded, exhausted, and overwhelmed. " 'Look here, Sam dear lad,' said Frodo: 'I am tired, weary, I haven't a hope left. But I have to go on trying to get to the Mountain, as long as I can move.' "[7]

Like Frodo, we feel we have given all that our hearts can bear. Like him, we plod through our spiritual practices because they are the hard assignment given us in the night. Like Frodo, we feel they're useless and pointless. But we must keep on keeping on.

Spiritual practices fuel us for the hard journey ahead. Just as Frodo arose each day and forced himself to journey onward, offering ourselves to God even when God seems absent enables us to arise, set our jaw, and walk into another dark day.

Because They Nurture Our Growth

In the award-winning television series *Joan of Arcadia*, teenaged Joan (Amber Tamblin) encounters God in an array of strange guises. God appears as a housewife, a myopic child, a chess player, a custodian, a drama teacher, and a Goth — complete with spiked hair, black lips, and several piercings (Goth God was my personal favorite!) — to name only a few. God's disguises catch Joan — and the viewer — off guard because we are unaccustomed to imagining God in such turnouts. It's not wrong; it's just...different.

When I am in a dark night, my way of knowing God flips over. It's most unsettling. Ever since I was a child, I have felt God's assuring presence inside me. But in the dark night, the inner light clicks off and I feel cold and lost. In these times I must look for God's presence outside: in the stately grace of a swan, in poignant music, in the faces of worshippers, in the embrace of my husband and children. I don't like this discipline — it feels foreign and disjointed. I want God back inside. Now.

On the other hand, someone who tends to approach God with her mind may find her head so clouded that she must open her hesitant heart. Faith, we discover in the night, is work. The dark night challenges us like nothing else to explore fresh ways to relate with God.

Because They Slow Us Down

Spiritual practices have the power to still us. Because the night is different from typical experience, we live differently during it. For one thing, we get still, and that's much harder than getting busy. Hence, the dark night feels wrong; what's the point of standing around in the dark accomplishing nothing? We've been trained to get out in the world and do God's work, but in the night such work feels forced. Our gears grind against each other; we screech to a dead halt.

Our society does not look kindly upon inactivity, for we associate stillness with laziness. The dark night calls us not to spiritual sloth, but to stronger discipline. Spiritual practices help us obey God's call to stand very still when we feel pressured to succumb to frantic activity.

Because We Love God

In spiritual practice we shout determined love to an absent God. Faithful practice expresses our faith and hope, even when faith is nearly dead and hope seems like an enemy. In the discipline of spiritual practice, we submit our will to God's without demanding attendant good feelings. We begin, in small incremental steps, to love God for God alone. Such naked intent rings through a wrenching prayer by Henri Nouwen: "I can only keep trying to be faithful, even though I feel faithless most of the time. What else can I do but keep praying to you, even when I feel dark; to keep writing about you, even when I feel numb; to keep speaking in your name, even when I feel alone. Come, Lord Jesus, come. Have mercy on me, a sinner. Amen."[8]

Spiritual practice is our chance to return God's unconditional love. Faithfulness in practice — despite our feelings — reveals our allegiance to God. We cling to the cross even as its splinters pierce our skin.

How Do I Begin?

God, the tailor, custom fits the dark night to each believer. Just as we relate to God out of our uniqueness, so we choose practices that call us by name. The books *Practicing Our Faith* and *Wisdom Distilled from the Daily*[9] offer an array of spiritual practices. Also, a few practices other dark night survivors employed to see them through are listed below. Feel free to sample them at will.

✝ We can practice a breath prayer. On the intake we can pray, "Not my will," and on the outtake, "Thine." Or we can pray on the intake, "All in God," and on the outtake, "God in all."

✝ We can picture our isolation, abandonment, hopelessness, and confusion in pen and ink, in paint on canvas, with fabric on a banner, with clay, or in whatever art form names our struggle.

✝ We can write simple, aching prayers or psalms of lament.

✝ We can employ a discipline of gratitude by writing a weekly thank-you note to someone who has befriended our journey. Before falling asleep, we might thank God for three specific blessings.

✝ We can create a litany in which we express our fear, bewilderment, and sense of desertion. Between each phrase we can repeat the words, "How long, O Lord?"

✝ Like Naomi, we can give ourselves a name that describes our experience of the night (Ruth 1:20–21). The name can remind us to be honest with God about our feelings and open to God's invisible work in our battered soul.

✝ We can seek out literature and films that connect with our night's journey. The silent film *Joan of Arc* is a stark and powerful companion.

✝ We can invite music into our night — whether we listen to it, sing, play an instrument, or compose. "Sometimes I Feel Like a Motherless Child," "When I Survey," "Pachelbel's Canon," "It Is Well with My Soul," and Handel's "Messiah" may speak to our suffering. The haunting song "Hallelujah," from the *Shrek* soundtrack (no kidding), is a great dark night song.

✝ We can take a blanket outside, lie in the dark, and notice our body's position in the stillness. We can note what comes to our awareness because of the night.

The dark night was a cod liver oil time, but, invisibly, those spiritual practices, like a good multivitamin, slowly strengthened my soul to bear more of God's weighty and glorious presence. My delight at dawn — which did come — was unspeakable. Joy — a deep, real, potent joy — came in the morning. *In the night, practices that keep us keeping on are vital — if tasteless. But what happens when the bottom drops out?*

COD LIVER OIL PRAYERS

I'm too angry to speak, Lord, but I yield to you my silence. Amen.

It's tasteless stuff, this prayer, worship, and Scripture reading. But I will do it today. Only today. One day at a time. Amen.

LIFELINES

In addition to the books already mentioned... *St. Benedict on the Freeway* by Corinne Ware: We can live a recollected life on the freeway! The author describes her work as the "popular mechanics of spirituality": down to earth, real, and daily. By golly, we can do this!

Prayer and Temperament by Chester Michael and Marie Norrisey: A great book with a hideous cover. Could someone get rid of the glaring yellow background and naked green man, please? Don't open your eyes until you look inside, where you'll find practices attuned to your spiritual type.

The Karate Kid directed by John Avildsen: Really! Just think of all those repetitive, boring tasks brutal Miyagi forced on that poor kid. "Wax on, wax off...."

The Shawshank Redemption directed by Frank Darabont: Wrong-fully convicted Andy Dufresne's (Tim Robbins) discipline and determination are cloaked until the movie's surprise ending. A truly memorable film; watch for its surprising baptism scene.

"The Wilderness" by Michael Card: Card is not an "I love Jesus, yea, yea, yea" musician. We can listen and listen again. "In the Wilderness" so accompanied my journey through the night that I played it near to death.

"When It's All Been Said and Done" by Robin Mark: Don't let its simplicity fool you. It's all in there — the reason we keep on keeping on.

The Gleaners by Jean-François Millet: Millet did a revolution-ary thing: he honored the common. The three women in the painting, solid and sweating in their homespun garb, have their own nobility. They are real, they are dignified, they do what must be done — they are us.

✛ *How Deep This Pit?* ✛

. . . my soul thirsts for you; my flesh faints for you, as in a dry and
weary land where there is no water.   — Psalm 63:1

So much in me had died and I'd no physical or emotional strength
to make a new beginning. Despairing thoughts absorbed my waking mind and riddled my fitful sleep. I was tumbling off a cliff.
Where was God?

David and the girls had plans for the evening; I sat alone with
the wretched night. Around me, the house darkened as evening
shadows inched over the windowsills and across the expanse of
living room. On our sofa, patterned in rich Southwest colors, I
felt myself grow smaller, paler, and more alone.

Always I had loved aloneness, indeed thirsted for it. In solitude
I felt God's comforting presence and imagined myself a small
child held in an enormous divine lap, safe arms encircling me.
A familiar voice close to my ear whispered away my soul's ache:
"Peace, child. I'm here."

But tonight, as I shrunk small and smaller on the sofa, no
voice offered comfort; no arms encircled my shivering form. I
was alone, quite alone, with the depression that had dogged me
since childhood and with tormenting memories of past wounds.
Despair, seeping through the very pores of my skin, had come to
claim me.

I rose from the couch, unable to bear my smallness and lostness in that wide-open shadowed room. Into the bedroom I
shuffled, and shut the door behind me. Leaning against its cold
rigidity, I looked around at the once-familiar clutter of furniture
and bedding. Still too much space for someone so small and lost.
I slipped into the master bathroom and pressed the door shut.
Here, at last, I could feel myself again.

Huddling in a corner, I began to shake and then, without warning, to scream. My souls' torment would be borne in silence no longer. I screamed like someone dying in agony, again and again as shadows turned to blackness. My throat went raw, but still the screams came, savage and determined. I, who had borne two hard labors in silence, found voice for a pain that seemed without promise.

What if the neighbors heard me and called for the paramedics? What would I say? What would they do? But it didn't matter. Screams rose to the surface and broke out of my body like a tide that would and must come. With my life as it stood, screaming was the only prayer I had to offer.

So I gave myself over to screams as one is lowered under the water in baptism, and I let them do the work my soul needed done.

By the time my family returned, the screams had done their work. I greeted them, exhausted but quiet. A stillness settled on my soul: no warmth, but a center of rest. It was not the last time depression or the night drove screams from my throat or shudders from my body. In those seasons, suffering poets from centuries past gave me comfort. I poured over their poems, feeling their ache afresh, finding friends who shared my pain. Here was language for my screams.

I drank in the psalmists' stark "faith in the trenches" poetry. Not a word of pretense or false pietism marred these hymns. And herein lay their haunting beauty, for the poets had laid bare their souls before God.

How long, O Lord? Will you forget me forever?

. . . if you are silent to me, I shall be like those who go down to the Pit.

My God, my God, why have you forsaken me? —Psalm 13:1, 28:1, 22:1

My heart sang its own lament in counterpoint. In those screaming hours, I lost all need to explain away the psalmists' despair
or rationalize their tormented feelings. I, too, owned those emotions. Like me, the psalmists expressed the emotions of a season.
Did the poet who penned *"My God, my God, why have you forsaken me?"* feel God had deserted him? I believe he did. Did he
believe God had deserted him? If so, why address the song to
God? I found in this poet's guileless expression of God's abandonment *to* God a courageous act of faith, one that surely touched
his Maker's heart.

Yet the psalmists' laments and my own screams stood in stark
contrast to what I'd witnessed in "respectable religion." The
psalmists' prayer language, raw with emotion, and my wordless screams contradicted what was deemed the proper way to
approach God. Even so, those screams in the night were the
truest prayers I ever uttered. I treasure the psalmists' expression
of agony every bit as much as their celebration poetry. For my
life is full of pain and praise. And I want God in the whole of it.

Dark Night or Depression?

Some of my screaming agony stemmed from the night, but some
came from another source. I wrote earlier of my lifelong struggle
with depression. Depression and the dark night look similar and
may occur at the same time, but they come from different places.

Depression results from a physical anomaly such as a genetic
predisposition or a disease that causes a chemical imbalance in
the brain, or from a psychological wound resulting from abuse
or catastrophe. Temperaments like mine tend toward depression.
Usually depression is a combination of these factors. Because
depression has a psychological and/or a physiological base, it
should be treated therapeutically and medically.

I suffered depression while journeying through the dark night because I was accustomed to God's comforting, indwelling presence. Suddenly, my warmed and malleable heart iced over. God, it appeared, had deserted me to a deep freeze. I felt sad, frightened, and hopeless.

But while depression is dangerous, the dark night is loving and wholesome. Depression may come to any person, but a prerequisite is required for the dark night: we must desire a relationship with God. Without such a desire, there is no dark night.

Contrasting Depression with the Dark Night

Depression	Dark Night
Originates in the body or psyche	Originates in God
Needs treatment	Needs to be endured
Imparts feelings of worthlessness	Imparts feelings of perplexity
Produces a sense of despair	Produces a sense of holding one's breath
Generates hopelessness	Generates anguished hope
Saps energy for and interest in prayer	Creates a yearning to pray even while feeling out of sync
Impairs ability to focus	Strengthens focus on relationship with God
Is destructive	Is wholesome[10]

For years I begged God to free me of depression. God chose instead to make my depression a powerful teacher — and a tremendous humbler! As we walk through the dark night and/or when we suffer depression, let's hold fast to this truth: neither the dark night nor depression is a symptom of faithlessness. Neither is cause for shame or guilt. Instead both, when given to God, are potent with possibility. For both bring us to a place of emptiness. The psalmists emptied their souls' ache into poetry. I emptied my soul in screams. When our trials exhaust us and pain strips us bare, we become a space ripe for filling. *However deep anguish plunges us, God is deeper still. But is it worth it to find out for ourselves?*

SCREAMING PRAYERS

Lord of the night, I hurt too much to construct a decent sentence. Here I am — hurt, bewildered, depressed, and angry — but I am yours. Amen.

Jesus, what love compelled you into suffering and aloneness? I haven't such a capacity. Have mercy. Amen.

LIFELINES

A Scent of Water by Elizabeth Grudge: It may take a trip to the library or secondhand bookshop to find this one, but it's worth it. Grudge's book is a baptism, especially for those who suffer from emotional or mental disease. A cleansing, hopeful read.

Reflections on the Psalms by C. S. Lewis: Lewis brings his sizeable literary skill, theological savvy, and winsome wit to this exploration of biblical poetry. My favorite passage: a child's poem on "chocolate eggs and Jesus risen."

What's Eating Gilbert Grape directed by Lasse Hallström: A perfect movie, to my mind, and a realistic portrayal of depression's cost to ourselves and to those nearest us. What happens when we give too little of ourselves — or too much?

The Hours directed by Stephen Daldry: The movie is a story trilogy, and I am thinking of the Virginia Woolf portion here. Nicole Kidman portrays the writer; we watch, sorrowing, as she battles depression and finally succumbs to suicide.

"The Edge" by Michael Card: Thank God for Michael Card and his honesty. In a time when Christianity all too often equals self-righteousness, Card sings frankly about suicidal ideation and wins my wholehearted esteem.

"Eleanor Rigby" by The Beatles: Can we think of a lonelier song? Do these people have anything left to live for, and don't we all wear a face that we keep "in a jar by the door"?

Scream by Edvard Munch: While on a walk, a sick, weary Munch felt a scream pulse through nature. In response, he painted a disturbing, entrancing, evocative work. It's not famous for nothing!

At Eternity's Gate by Vincent van Gogh: Van Gogh eloquently, poignantly, captures a moment most of us have visited at least once.

✠ *Toward the Tomb* ✠

Darkness invades the afternoon sky. In a final act of reckless faith, Jesus entrusts His spirit — His entire being — to an absent Father. He gives up everything. Every thing. Now we stand, hushed and open, in the mouth of a cave. Listen. Is someone whispering our name?

PRAYERS OF SUFFERING

Jesus, it is our deepest honor to suffer alongside you: with children who ache for tenderness, with teens whose only companion is loneliness, with workers who endure mind-numbing jobs to provide for their families, with parents who stand baffled before their children's graves. Whatever it takes, strengthen us that we may accompany your suffering with our own. Amen.

I can't stop crying, Jesus. Weep with me. Amen.

My God, my God, why have you forsaken me?

CHAPTER FIVE

A RELINQUISHING DEATH

He was cut off from the land of the living.
—Isaiah 53:8

For to me, living is Christ and dying is gain.
—Philippians 1:21

Affliction makes God appear to be absent for a time, more absent than a dead man, more absent than light in the utter darkness of a cell.
—Simone Weil, *Waiting on God*

Then Joseph bought a linen cloth, and taking down the body, wrapped it in the linen cloth, and laid it in a tomb that had been hewn out of the rock. He then rolled a stone against the door of the tomb.
—Mark 15:46

How long have we been crying? Our faces are wet with tears. In silence, we follow the body from cross to tomb. How gently the faithful lower him; how tenderly they wrap him in linen; with what devotion they lay him upon the stone slab. He is beyond its chill now. We lie down beside him, feeling the cold eat away all life we once claimed as our own. Our self-will seeps out as the chill creeps in. Less and less do we think of ourselves as separate selves. More and more are we drawn to the pale linen-wrapped figure beside us until night encloses all and we know no more.

There is a certain peace in the grave — nothing to plan for, nothing to stew over. A final yielding that leaves us limp enough to simply be. No need, we find, to create an uplifting ending for a tragic story. It is enough to dwell in the tomb of today.

In the tomb we relinquish our drive to push God along, to take the initiative, to be proactive. The time will come for action, but Holy Saturday is our time of letting go. It becomes enough to simply belong to God.

For there are things God invites us to yield to death — not because they are bad, but because, simply because, God asks us to. The tomb invites us into the ultimate act of faith: the willingness to die without expecting to receive in return exactly what we'd wanted in the first place. Unless we die to what we want for ourselves, God cannot transform us. Resurrection carries always an element of surprise and wonder. We must close our eyes — no peeking, now! — and let God lay to rest in us whatever God wills.

We yield ourselves to death. Period. No expectations. No holding out.

And leave the resurrection business to God.

Night falls on Saturday and on our quiet form. We breathe our last and lie in holy death.

—⟋m⟍—

Summer is a season of frantic pace in children's ministry: Vacation Bible School, camp after camp after camp, special children's programs, then straight into promotion and a new church year. Yet during the last summer of a ministry position, I had the sensation of being trapped in slow motion. Each activity unfolded with excruciating clarity and deliberation as a voice inside my head intoned: "Last time. Last time." At each program's completion, I turned back to see a mammoth, steel-gray vault door swinging slowly, relentlessly closed. As an invisible hand pressed the door home with a resounding clang, a tremor went straight through to my bones.

My work was done. I submitted my resignation, finished my degree, and waited for God to lead me to the next ministry position. After all, I had followed as led; God would take care of me. I pulled together my résumé and sent it out. Opportunities blossomed with possibility, then withered, died, and blew away with the wind. Every step I took forward in faith seemed only a dream step, requiring mammoth effort but taking me nowhere. Nowhere at all.

When I saw people about town, they would ask what was going on with me. I could see the disappointment in their eyes when I reported that I was still waiting. Friends wandered away, and my life, once a fury of activity, became quite small and solitary. At the same time, the publishing house for which I had been writing went under, and I lost even my small writing career. What was I now? Who was I?

My plans for doing what I believed I'd been called to do began to take their last shuddering breaths. All my future dreams were slowly, slowly dying. Months ticked by as I lay gasping in my own Holy Saturday tomb. My hopes and expectations of a ministry position had to die, that much I knew. But why? Why give me a desire and an ability, then not provide a place? How could I bear to live and not serve as called?

Was I not to live by faith and hope? Yes. But that faith, that hope, resided wholly in what God had called me to long ago. On the day the preacher came to visit, I perched on the sofa's arm. On the day the preacher came, I said yes to following Jesus. My first and final call is to exercise a reckless, wholehearted love for my Lord. To let that be enough. If God required, I would relinquish even my dreams of serving as I'd hoped, letting my willingness, my availability to serve be enough.

Why those hard images of slamming vault doors and uncompromising commands? What I experienced as sternness from God, I now recognize as the tender leading of a parent who knows a daughter better than she knows herself. Only the starkest of images would compel me to release long-held commitments. It was time for my old life to die — time for me to sleep the soundless sleep that precedes resurrection.

A hush falls over the tomb. We are beyond expectation, but around us the host of heaven holds its collective breath. Each second the great transformation ticks closer. Wait — do you see a strand of light on the gray horizon?

✠ *Will God Take Me Under?* ✠

It is a fearful thing to fall into the hands of the living God.
— Hebrews 10:31

I nestled all the angles of my thirteen-year-old body between the sheets and closed my eyes. I'd spent the day at church: Sunday School, morning worship, Church Training, evening worship. My mind was full of the things of God.

Sleep had washed its first gentle waves over me when I jarred awake and upright. My upstairs room looked the same as ever — same window, same ceiling light, same wood flooring — but I was not the same. For the first time in my life, I realized I was mortal. I could fall asleep and never again wake. In the morning, my parents could find my cold body.

Sweat beaded my brow and I could hear, in the night's stillness, my ragged, terrified breath. Lying back against my pillow, I spread my fingers before my face, feasting in the silhouette of their presence. I pressed a hand against my chest, relieved to feel my heart's rhythmic beat. Knowing I could die made me aware that I lived. And I wanted to live. For hours I lay awake, a sentinel against the death that might come with sleep. My teenaged body begged for rest, but I fought it back. I would not be caught unaware.

Then I knew, quite suddenly, that my efforts were pointless, even laughable. God was in charge of my death just as God nurtured my life. Did I trust, really trust God?

The question had not come from me. God whispered into my young heart, "Do you trust me, Kaye? Really trust me? Then sleep, child, in my care."

Drifting into slumber, I knew I'd given up something — and that the choice to relinquish it meant I was growing. But it also felt like being lost alone on an ocean.

Years passed, and then the soul night fell on me. Once again, I was cast upon the waters of God's sovereignty. Throughout my life, I'd found solace in the beauty of words. Pain and delight would find me at my journal pouring words — glorious words! — onto the page. Although sometimes I chose not to write because I couldn't bear to see my anguish staring up at me in permanent black and white, writer's block was a foreign concept. I knew that I depended entirely on God for my writing; if I prayed, if I toughed it out for a few hours, the juices would flow and so would the words.

The worst of the night left me wordless. I felt like a child struggling through a fifty-word essay on her summer vacation: "It was very, very, very, very nice." The Holy Spirit, on whom my writing utterly depended, had gone silent. I received nothing, which is precisely what I felt like.

The truth I'd known in my head — that I'm lost without and entirely dependent on God — flooded my soul. How terrifying it would be if God were not loving and good! Just now God seemed determined to destroy me. I'd been cast upon the waves of God's sovereignty, and I was sinking.

In this time of tumbling, a friend invited me to join some fellow seminarians for a movie night. I eagerly agreed and saw, for the first time, Tom Hank's portrayal in *Cast Away.* So profoundly did the movie capture my experience that when it ended I could barely speak. The images teased and troubled my soul; I rented the film and watched it again. One scene in particular ached with the truth of my experience: a scene in the dead of night.

High-powered FedEx executive Chuck Noland (Tom Hanks) finds himself one moment in the washroom of a transcontinental aircraft and the next entombed in the wrecked plane as it sinks into the stormy ocean. He inflates a raft and follows it to the surface, where nature's wild cacophony — screeching wind, thundering waves, black night, and shocks of lightning — rage against him. He struggles aboard the small, yellow raft, grabs its oar, and glances around at the ocean. One look at the tiny paddle beside the monstrous sea and Chuck tosses it aside — useless. He simply lies down, grabs hold of the raft, and lets the ocean have its wild way. A tremendous wave hovers just above the raft; salt water deluges the small vessel, but Chuck hangs on and stays afloat.

Torrents of rain spear him from above while the fathomless chilling ocean numbs him from below. The plane and all the security of Chuck's past sink with a groan, leaving him to the ocean's mercy.

The yellow raft becomes the ocean's toy, riding the waves, lost in obscurity. Interminable blackness settles on the merciless sea, then the sound of pelting rain. A sudden shaft of lightning illumines a jagged stone just as it pierces the raft's skin. Chuck scrambles blindly from the wounded raft and onto the safety of land. The ocean has delivered him.

John of the Cross gave name to the wild ride; he called it the Night of the Spirit.[11]

Undertow

To this point, we have dipped our toes in the night, experiencing what John of the Cross called the Night of the Senses.[12] In the Night of the Senses, God allows us some illusion of self-sufficiency. In the Night of the Senses, we delude ourselves into believing that our oars can tackle the ocean, that we have resources other than God to fall back on. We never say so, of course, even to ourselves, but we think we needn't trust God *entirely*, after all. We are children playacting faith.

In the Night of the Spirit we feel the undertow. God whisks away all our delusions; we are cast adrift on God's incalculable ocean. Driven along by God's sovereignty in the dead of night, a new terror awakens: what if God is not good?

For the first time we've an idea of what words like omni-present, omniscient, and omnipotent mean. And we've a fearful inkling of what futile, powerless, and frail might mean. We are cast adrift, and there's not one thing we can do about it. What will become of us?

Why Take the Plunge?

The dark night is a violent ride. Why put ourselves through it? We enter the night when, in our longing for God, we cast aside all caution. Only an agony of yearning will spur us to enter, for we fear we'll lose all our security — including our very sense of self.

Yes, we've lost control; the currents of God's will are bearing us away in the dark. But thanks to the night, our direction is surer than ever, for, in our blindness, we let God steer. It's hard to trust God not to abandon us to an undertow or dash us against the rocks. In the night, we cannot see God's intents. But we will. In the morn, we will. So in the wildness of the Night of the Spirit, we cling to Chuck's raft on the raging ocean and, in the end, we come to know that God is sovereign — and that God is love. *Adrift on God's sovereignty, we've swallowed some ocean and felt our smallness. How long must we hang on and ride it out?*

Prayers on the Ocean

I thought a safety net hung beneath my faith, God. I see now that if you are not love, I am truly lost. Amen.

You are too wild and reckless for my smallness, Lord. But I would rather be destroyed by you than live with anyone else. Amen.

You've whisked away the props and sets, God. I stand alone on reality's barren stage. Do you care? Amen.

I'm hanging on as best I can, Lord. Don't make it too long. Amen.

LIFELINES

 Jane Eyre by Charlotte Brontë: From earliest childhood, Jane's life mirrored the bleak, wild English countryside that nearly took her life. Forced to choose between the one person who loved and valued her and living Godward, Jane threw herself out into the wild cold.

Dark Night of the Soul by John of the Cross: Mirabai Starr's translation of the classic sings with John's poetic voice. A commentary on his dark night poem, it bids us hurl ourselves into God's waves.

Cast Away directed by Robert Zemeckis: Just one last word on the film: Wilson's my favorite!

"Pachelbel's Canon" by Johann Pachelbel: I first heard this piece in *Ordinary People*—another movie about ocean fury. Pachelbel's work calms us, even as we trust to the waves. We may feel we're adrift, but, in the words of another writer, *"Don't panic!"*

The Great Wave by Katsushika Hokusai: Majestic and towering, captured at high crest, the great wave dwarfs all boats below. Though it hovers at the pinnacle of destruction, to wish this wave tamer would somehow diminish us as well.

✠ *How Long, O Lord?* ✠

*And let endurance have its full effect, so that you may be mature and
complete, lacking in nothing.* —James 1:4

"Breathe!" intoned the childbirth instructor. A covey of pregnant
women sat on the floor, leaning against our respective spouses.

"The most important thing to remember in labor is your
breathing." So we learned to take a deep breath, hold it for ten
counts, and let it out, and we practiced panting. At the time, practicing to breathe felt a bit ludicrous — we all were pregnant with
our first children and had no notion what awaited us.

David and I had waited five years for our first child, then nearly
lost her in the fourth month of pregnancy; I determined to cover
all my bases. I read every childbirth book I could get my hands
on, purchased cloth diapers to save money and the environment,
and played music for and read stories to my unborn daughter. I
was going to do this thing right, by golly!

Labor began the day before Arielle was due with what felt like
a severe backache.

"It'll get much worse than this before it's over," was the nurse's
prophecy of doom. She was right.

Hour after hour passed as the pain slowly escalated. I had not
dilated one bit. We'd practiced our breathing and relaxation ex-
ercises in class while our husbands made eye contact with us and
reminded us to breathe. With back labor, David stood behind
me, pressing the heels of his hands into my back.

"Harder!" I begged, feeling no relief. I carried the bruises for
weeks. I was no match for the agony of back labor. Things were
definitely not going as planned.

Twenty-plus hours into labor, the intensity shot off the map:
transition had come. In transition, pain intensifies until its power

blocks out everything except the life it is urging toward birth. I kept on breathing; it was the best thing I could do for the child and for myself.

Arielle arrived backward, with the umbilical cord wrapped around her neck. She looked like a Wedgwood doll: perfectly formed and completely blue. The doctor whipped away the cord, and the blue gave way to a rosy pink. Minutes later, my daughter gazed up at me, her eyes filled with wisdom and wonder. I was a mother.

Six years later, we sat in another childbirth class. The instructor promised me I'd not have back labor this time because the child was positioned properly. She lied. But, like the first coach, she gave good advice: breathe!

My water broke in the night and back labor began, at first mildly and then wildly. By the time I'd been admitted and checked, my body's instincts took over. A single rational question scuttled through my mind: "Can anyone endure this much pain and retain her sanity?" I recall lowering myself onto all fours in the hospital corridor while white trousers scurried from all directions to check my vitals. Once again, hours of pain produced no dilation.

The hospital bent some rules and let me enter a whirlpool. Sinking into the water, I counseled myself, "Breathe!" As I relaxed, transition came almost immediately. Bethany nearly arrived before I could make it to the birthing chair and while the doctor was still pulling on her gloves. This child, all buoyancy and challenge, was and is her own mystery.

Transition is something that happens *to* a woman during labor. We don't get ourselves comfortable, select a convenient time, and announce, "Okay, I believe I will now begin transition." Instead, the stage of labor unfolds in God's time. The best we can do is stay out of the way. Interestingly, our major role in transition is to breathe. In the night we stay awake and alive to what is being born in us, but, much as we'd like to, we can't force things along.

Like me, many women experience transition as the dark time in labor. Our focus goes inside, to the life struggling to find its way out. Frankly, during the time of transition, many of us would like to rethink our options. Maybe having a baby wasn't such a good idea after all.

Of course, it's too late to turn back and, one way or another, our baby finds its way into the world. And then, we, too, are reborn.

Although we have more choices about entering the dark night than we have about entering labor's transition, in both cases God bears us to a place where we become someone new. In childbirth, the pain women suffer for a baby creates a deep bond; in the night, our suffering bonds us to God, for we realize nothing can fill our souls but the one who created them. We emerge from labor's transition into the stage of pushing with new resolve to get this thing done; we emerge from the dark night with new resolve to make God our one and only desire.

Some labors are short; some seem interminable. We grit our teeth and make our way through. Can we know how long this laborious night will last? How long must we keep breathing?

What's Taking So Long?

The length of a dark night varies — usually lasting for several years. "The mind has been plunged into darkness," John of the Cross writes. "This darkness will last as long as it needs to pull the mind up out of those old ruts it has been stuck in for so long."[13] He then lists factors that affect the night's duration.

The first factor concerns our soul's resilience. Can we stay put in the night or do we need frequent breaks? There's no issue of shame here. The question simply concerns our spiritual makeup; God knows what we need. Our sole purpose is to endure the night. We needn't bother to suffer more nobly than our neighbor does!

Second, the amount of cleansing our soul needs affects our night's length. How long will it take God to transform our root passions? Third, the night's depth and intensity bears upon its length. Is our soul best purged and kindled by a slow, steady flame or by the sudden ferocity of a blowtorch? God adapts the flame to provide each individual soul with its best curative kindling.

To John's three factors, I respectfully add two, which I base both on personal experience and on interviews with others who endured the night. The night's tenure is lengthened if we get stuck or if we have suffered wounds to our soul.

Evangelicals, like myself, can get stuck early in the night when guilt over not doing enough for God dogs our every step. Why? Although we preach and teach grace, our practice tends to be guilt and works oriented. We believe the remedy for guilt is increased work for God. In our frenzied efforts to measure up, we miss God's invitation to be still and listen. Thus, we can spend years enduring the night's initial ravages. The more we strive to work ourselves out of it, the more distraught we become. But if we respect our incarnation enough to balance work with rest and reflection, we can attend to God and be moved through the night.

A wound to our soul violates our entire being, for our soul is who we are. In response to such wounding we might feel anger, terror, shame, hopelessness, or even self-loathing. Soul crimes can take the form of physical, mental, emotional, or sexual abuse. Shaming tactics such as ostracizing or minimizing and religious teachings designed to manipulate the learner also violate souls. A soul attack is especially destructive when perpetrated by persons we associate with God.

But why should violations perpetrated by others lengthen our night's tenure? For those who suffer soul wounds, the length of a night can be as much about excising scar tissue as it is about purging sin. "But that's not fair!" we protest. Why should we suffer over violence visited on us by others? When I ask such questions, God draws my mind to two courageous sufferers: Victor Frankl and Julian of Norwich.

Frankl, who suffered internment as a Jew in a Nazi concentration camp, wrote a book chronicling its horrors. The second half of *Man's Search for Meaning* posits an approach to psychotherapy based on the premise that we can endure any suffering in which we find meaning. From the crucible of his own abuse, Frankl created hope for his fellow humans. That's my idea of a hero.

Earlier, in the fourteenth century, Julian of Norwich, England, suffered the last stages of a terminal illness. She was thirty. As Julian neared death, she received sixteen "showings" of Christ dying and of Christ risen. The dying Julian asked Jesus hard questions about sin and suffering. When the showings ended, Julian recovered. For the next twenty years she pondered the meaning of her visions, then compiled them into a book. God never discounts sin and suffering, Julian assures her readers, but God promises us that in the end, "All shall be well, and all shall be well, and all manner of things shall be well."[14]

Strangely dark-night pain can work miracles in our wounded souls. Its ravages transport us to a place of deep peace and even gratitude. All *shall* be well. But it takes time and we mustn't give up. *We are in for the duration, however long that may be. But however can we survive?*

Birthing Prayers

The night hurts so much we want to take over and make it stop, Lord. Tell us what to do. Amen.

Help us believe you are bringing something wondrous to life in us, God, for our hope is dead. Amen.

Give us strength to forgive even the unforgivable, Lord, that you might truly set us free. Amen.

LIFELINES

 Showings or *The Revelation of Divine Love* by Julian of Norwich: These are the same book, essentially, though the old English versions may have you hating Julian before you're through. Find a readable copy and feel Julian's arms go round you, giving assurance that "all shall be well."

The Elephant Man directed by David Lynch: Rated R for intensity and filmed entirely in black and white, the film's opening special effects are dated, but once the actors take their places that's all forgotten. We might label those who endure abuse with grace "outdated" or "masochistic" were it not for the example of John Merritt — the elephant man.

"I Know Who Holds Tomorrow" by Ira Stanphill: This is a great shower song! I sang it over and over, with tears and suds washing down my face. It got me through the day — and the Night.

"The Sound of Silence" by Simon and Garfunkel: Silence is loud in the night. We, too, seek God's voice in dangerous, unexplored places.

Pietà by Michelangelo: People weep when they stand before it. Though I've seen the Pietà only in books, it wrenches my heart and I can't tear my eyes from that stunned, desolate maternal face. However did Mary endure?

✣ *Has God Walked Away?* ✣

So if anyone is in Christ, there is a new creation: everything old has passed away; see, everything has become new! — 2 Corinthians 5:17

My hope was dead, my life confused, my soul frozen in pain, and God took a holiday.

I doggedly kept up my practice of praying as I walked, though the walks offered no balm for my tortured soul. And so it was on this day. Weighted with sorrow, my shoes dragged slower and slower until I stopped dead still in the middle of the trail. Overcome with despair, I found my way to a nearby bench and sat — I've no idea how long.

My head dropped into my hands. I silently begged God to return; my entreaty met only cold silence. Anger swept through me; I nearly choked with it. How dare my Creator take such advantage of my powerlessness! What kind of God would desert his own child?

Hot, desperate tears burned my eyes.

Then I had a sense of being watched.

I raised my head and lifted my eyes. Before me stood a boy — about eleven years old, I'd say — and his large, happy dog. I knew the child had been standing there for some time, waiting.

The boy looked directly into my eyes. "Hi," he said, his voice bright with hope and delight.

A smile found my face. "Hi," I responded.

With one last smile and a wag from the dog's tail, the two departed.

"Are you a child or an angel?" I asked his retreating back. "Whoever you are, I know Who sent you."

It was a long time before I again felt God's indwelling, continuous presence. During the waiting time, however, God kept sending calling cards: invitations to hang on, like the boy and his dog. I had only to open my eyes and my imagination; God turned up in some intriguing places.

Art Calling Cards

I stared at the tiny textbook print of Caravaggio's *The Supper at Emmaus,* drinking in the fresh colors of fruit, fowl, and bread, surveying the play of light and shadow across table and wall, memorizing the attitude of each figure.

The painting, which portrays the Emmaus meal (Luke 24:13–35), pulses with energy. One startled figure thrusts arms wide in disbelief. Another figure's arms push against his chair as he shoots to his feet. Even the bowl of fruit, perched precariously on table's edge, vibrates with excitement. I wanted to lunge forward and catch it. Jesus, framed within a triangle of figures, light falling upon his serene face, reaches a hand toward me.

Caravaggio believed. He believed enough to take brush in hand, and, with a palette of colored oils, paint living faith onto a canvas. His painting pulsates truth. Caravaggio had painted a calling card.

In the same way, God called to me through the music of contemporary Christian singer Michael Card. In both lyrics and melody, his songs "In the Wilderness" and "God's Own Fool" were God's siren calls in the night. Music's mystery, with its cadences and dynamics, reached me through night's shadow. Indeed, art, of all kinds, proved to be a potent calling card. In the night, I attended art shows, listened to music, read and read and read.

Creation Calling Cards

The man whispered, "God, speak to me."
And a meadowlark sang. But the man did not hear.

So the man yelled, "God, speak to me!"
Thunder rolled across the sky. But the man did not listen.

The man looked around and said, "God, let me see you."
A star shone brightly. But he noticed it not.

And the man shouted, "God, show me a miracle."
And a life was born. But the man was unaware.

So the man cried out in despair, "Touch me, God, and let
me know that you are here!"

Whereupon God reached down and touched the man.
But the man brushed the butterfly away and walked on.

— Author unknown[15]

When God seems absent or even dead, we can turn our senses toward creation. We can smell the pungent aroma of pine or the homey scent of coffee perking, we can savor the crunch of fresh fruit and vegetables, watch lightning illumine the night sky, feel a tree's bark and a cat's sensuous fur, listen to the wind's wail and the laughter of running water. In the night, we might not feel pleasure in these activities, but we can recognize in them proofs of God's continuing creative activity. Is it possible to stroke the velvet of a rose petal and believe God is not loving?

We can count on it: a seed's autumn burial will sprout in spring life — we live in a resurrection world. What tiny seed, shivering in the frozen soil, imagines itself transformed into a fresh world as a vibrant, stately plant? Nature's calling card assures us that we will emerge from the night as new creations.

Milestone Calling Cards

"Draw a line across your paper," instructed my professor. "Now mark it by decades. This is the timeline of your life. Above the line, write in events you experienced as spiritual highs. Below the line, write in the spiritual valleys." We scribbled away. Then she said, "Now, beside each experience, write in something you learned."

Sometimes looking back gives us strength to move forward. Strugglers across the centuries have found it so. I came to call the practice of remembering "milestones" (Psalm 77:11–12). In a milestones practice, we mark occasions of God's clear and present work. The psalmists, in their milestones practice, recounted God's action at the Red Sea crossing, God's wilderness provision, God's gift of the Promised Land. Jesus recognized the practice in the words, "Do this in remembrance of me." In like manner, I marked occasions of God's activity in the rough and tumble of my life. It helped me to hang on.

When we are in the midst of the dark night, we want to feel better any way we can. We want it to end *now*. God's calling cards invite us to hang on, but how can we when we are at our tether's end? Christian mystic and activist Simone Weil gives potent reason to grit our teeth and endure (italics mine): "Affliction makes God appear to be absent for a time, more absent than a dead man, more absent than light in the utter darkness of a cell. A kind of horror submerges the whole soul. During this absence there is nothing to love.... The soul has to go on loving in the emptiness, or at least to go on wanting to love.... Then, one day,

God will come to show himself to this soul and to reveal the beauty of the world to it, as in the case of Job. *But if the soul stops loving it falls, even in this life, into something almost equivalent to hell.*"[16]

The dark night may feel like hell, but giving up has far more destructive consequences. Let us do whatever we must to remain stone cold in the grave with Jesus until Easter morning comes to claim us. But, whatever we do, let us stay put. Our task in the dark night is to endure it. The greatest tragedy of all is to give up too soon. In doing the timeline activity, our class discovered that we had learned more from our times of spiritual desolation than we had from our mountaintop experiences. Yet more reason to hang on. *So we're encouraged to ride out the night. But what if we just want it all to stop so we can get off?*

CALLING CARD PRAYERS

Are you a magician, God, that you have disappeared? Take another form, surprise me however you like, but please, please reappear. Amen.

I want my children to know you through your actions across the centuries and in the lives of countless, beloved people. Help me teach them so that, in remembering, they might trust you with their todays. Amen.

Open my eyes, God, and my ears, and nose and mouth. Bring my skin to life that I might feel and see and hear and smell and taste you in every moment. Amen.

I can't hang on. God. Please, then, hang on to me. Amen.

LIFELINES

Walking on Water by Madeleine L'Engle: In my favorite book on faith and art, L'Engle finds God's calling cards lying about all over the place. Read it with your highlighter handy!

The Practice of the Presence of God by Brother Lawrence: This tiny classic explores the homespun wisdom of a man who cherished God as fully at the scullery sink as he did in the monastery chapel.

Joan of Arcadia produced by Barbara Hall: From Joan's feisty retorts to God, to the fine acting, to the television show's in the trenches wisdom, this is a class act. There's no "saccharine kills" religiosity here (available on DVD).

"What a Wonderful World" by Louis Armstrong: Nobody sings it like Satchmo. His voice — earthy, graveled, grounded — including the "dark, sacred night" in creation's blessings assures me that even this is as it should be.

"My Lord Is Near Me" by Barbara Fowler Gaultney: I grew up on this one; its soaring melody and powerful storm imagery sent my imagination into orbit. Listen with the lights out.

Black Iris III by Georgia O'Keeffe: Dark, beautiful, and brooding, O'Keeffe's painting awakens a yearning in us to see the world as she does. Look deeply at her painting and you will look more deeply at the world.

✠ *Journey to Nowhere?* ✠

For we walk by faith, not by sight.
— 2 Corinthians 5:7

I love going to the airport. After parking in the cheap seat lot, I can hike across miles of asphalt and arrive at the world's lowest-priced theme park — complete with rides! Believe it or not, I still get a kick out of sending my luggage chugging along the conveyor belt, catching the tram, and, on occasion, hopping aboard one of those tiny carts and whizzing along as wide-eyed pedestrians jump aside.

My favorite airport attraction is the moving sidewalk. I love watching people as they prepare to climb aboard. Some struggle to look dignified as the belt whisks their feet from beneath them; others dip a hesitant toe toward the moving mass as if to check its temperature. I know the feeling — the moment I step foot aboard I falter, resisting the need to relinquish my sense of balance and movement to the sidewalk's dictates. The airport's moving sidewalk — with two crucial differences — depicts our movement through the night.

As we step onto the throbbing sidewalk, a steel wall rises from the floor before us. We can feel its rigid chill as it coasts along, blocking our view and preventing our movement forward. The dark night is a passive experience for the soul; we can't step lively and hurry it up. Then, once the wall comes up, everything goes black. We strain our eyes to see something — even the outline of the handrail or the silhouette of our trembling fingers, but no. The darkness in which we're stranded is opaque.

As the floor rumbles unsteadily beneath our feet and our fingers slip along the handrails, our heart races in panic. Does the terminal toward which we'd headed really, indeed, exist? Nothing seems real in the vast darkness except our own lostness. Every sense we relied on before has failed us. We feel only cold steel against our trembling fingers and the awkward beating of our lonely heart. The point, we know, is to stay on the path, to hang tight and to hang in. If we can hold our footing in this dark and silent place, the sidewalk will do the rest.

But it's so hard to stay put on the sidewalk that we sometimes duck under the handrail and head off to scout around for a plate of nachos or a recent best seller. Because we want to feel better now (and who wouldn't?), we exchange our intended destination for instantaneous relief. But everything short of relationship with God proves second-rate and tawdry. Our hearts know nothing else will satisfy. God has ruined that for us already.

Thankfully, it's impossible to stay lost, for the entire airport belongs to God. The minute we edge our way back to the monorail, the journey picks up where we left off: we step onto the solitary sidewalk, another wall comes up, and we are, once again, on our way.

Through a quote on a web site, I met another journeyer who experienced the night as movement. Sensing a kindred spirit, I found her autobiography and read it in one sitting. Her story fills me with wonder.

Therese's Tunnel[17]

Therese, a profoundly sensitive and dedicated young nun, experienced the night as a tunnel. She was born to doting parents in 1873 in Alençon, France. Therese had a precocious yearning to serve God, which was to sustain her through tragedies to come. Before Therese turned five, her mother died of breast cancer. Her older sister, Pauline, raised Therese as her own.

A few years after the mother's death, Pauline left the family to take vows as a nun. Pauline's departure drove Therese into such despair, the child nearly died. Her family prayed over and tenderly cared for the bedridden child. As her body began to heal, Therese's soul began a journey toward maturity. More and more, the growing child turned toward God.

As a young teen, Therese felt an intense call to pray God's healing on lost souls. On one occasion, she prayed for a thief and murderer named Pranzini. Condemned to death, the convict showed no signs of repentance; Therese continued to intercede. Never did the murderer show remorse. Just before his execution, however, the man asked for a crucifix. He kissed it three times, then laid his head in the guillotine.

More than anything, Therese longed to become a nun. The Mt. Carmel convent considered her, at age fifteen, too young, and thus declined her request. Determined, Therese appealed up the ecclesiastical ladder all the way to the pope; still she was made to wait. At long last permission came; an ecstatic Therese entered the Carmelite convent. Faithfully, she followed her call to pray for the lost and to humbly serve the other nuns. But shortly after Therese entered the life for which she'd yearned, the torments came. Through a protracted dark night, she retained hope that her "impenetrable darkness" was indeed a gift from Jesus: "He [Jesus] allowed my soul to be overrun by an impenetrable darkness, which made the thought of heaven, hitherto so welcome, a subject of nothing but conflict and torment. And this trial was not to be a matter of a few days or a few weeks; it was to last until the moment when God should see fit to remove it.

"And that moment hasn't come yet.... I wish I could put down what I feel about it, but unfortunately that isn't possible; to appreciate the darkness of this tunnel, you have to have been through it...."[18]

Therese's darkness gnawed at her faith, tearing at her most comforting beliefs: "I hear its [her darkness's] mocking accents: '... You really believe, do you, that the mist which hangs about you will clear away later on?... death will make nonsense of your hopes; it will only mean a night darker than ever, the night of mere non-existence.'"[19]

Why would a young woman, barely out of her teens, ponder heaven with such determined hope? Thanks to superiors who ordered Therese to pen her autobiography, we know. Young Therese was dying of tuberculosis. As the disease progressed, Therese endured bleeding, fever, and a pain so intense it drove her to thoughts of suicide. Therese wrote until her weakened fingers could no longer grasp a pencil. Her final lines express her humility and devotion, but also her determined faith in God. "I fly to him [God] on the wings of confidence and of love...."[20]

Therese died at age twenty-four. Upon its publication, her autobiography, *The Story of a Soul*, swept the world. Therese's simple honesty and her daily, real-life faith sing through the story. The young nun died eager to see her beloved face to face, through the tunnel at last.

Like Therese, faith's adventure can lead us into the deepest caverns of despair—into holes so deep and black we cannot even sense Jesus' presence, into places so lost and dark we can find no way out. And that is when we stand quite still and say, *"Here am I,"* knowing that Jesus' promise, *"I am with you always"* is not swayed by our perceptions. Then we begin to see a step on the path ahead—just one step, then another. And when we, at last, step once again, blinking into full sunlight, we are blinded by the sheer joy of it all. Never before were trees this green with spring sparkle! Never did the wind so fill our lungs with life! Never were we so eager to walk out into the vibrancy of it all! Easter has found us!

In the night I felt I'd come to a standstill, but, in truth, God was moving me with more surety than my feeble steps could ever muster. God's tunnel, God's sidewalk, cannot fail. If we but hang on, God will take us through the night straight into God's heart. All we need do is climb aboard, plant our feet, and wait out the ride. (See Appendix C for John of the Cross's metaphor for the night as movement toward God.) *God is moving us through death into resurrection surprise. What is dying in us? And what is springing to life?*

PRAYERS IN THE TUNNEL

Lord of the night, help me to trust that you are drawing me home, though I feel I am trapped at a standstill. My confused determination to hang on and wait out the night is all I have to offer. Amen.

I need your guiding hand most, God, when I can feel it the least. Amen.

It's dark here, Lord, and I am no longer sure of my destination. Keep me safe, for I am deeply afraid. Amen.

LIFELINES

Hinds' Feet on High Places by Hannah Hurnard and *Pilgrim's Progress* by John Bunyan: Okay, I admit it, I like *Hinds' Feet* better than Bunyan's *Pilgrim's Progress,* which, while it amazes and inspires me, also depresses me. Bunyan's utterly male writing depicts the entire Christian journey as aloneness, struggle, and pain, and God comes across as punitive. Hurnard weaves occasions of blissful communion with Much Afraid's loving Shepherd into her sorrowful, hopeful story. Hurnard's allegory is underread and underappreciated in my view. And Bunyan is, of course, wonderful: just pull on your soul armor before reading.

The Ascent of Mount Carmel by John of the Cross: It's mystical and powerful and all the stuff that takes my breath away. John knows we're headed somewhere good.

Stars Wars I-VI produced by George Lucas: Lucas says the two trilogies are all one movie. Looked at as a whole, *Star Wars* is really about detachment; the TIE Starfighters and light sabers just make the viewing more fun! Remember when Luke had to take out the Death Star? He let go of all technological aids and simply relied on the force. And how did that work?

"Road to Zion" by Petra: In this ballad about journey, both melody and lyrics compel, especially the stanza about shadow.

"Precious Lord, Take My Hand" by Thomas Dorsey and George Allen: Dorsey wrote "Precious Lord" in the grief-stricken season following his wife's and his newborn son's deaths. Slow and woe-filled, "Precious Lord" is timeless.

"Jesus Walked that Lonesome Valley" arranged by William Levi Dawson: Another great spiritual. Jesus, too, made this sojourn, so even my aloneness is accompanied.

The Return of the Prodigal by Rembrandt: Henri Nouwen's book *The Return of the Prodigal Son* brilliantly explores this painting. Both book and painting remind us that we are headed home.

✠ *Toward Resurrection* ✠

Holy Saturday sinks into a night that is rich in black mystery. Challenged to trust our very spirits to God — even unto their death — we lay in the sealed chamber's stillness as night gathers.

It is the night of turning, a night pregnant with creative energy. Around us and within our inert bodies, transforming powers surge: preparing the miracle, awaiting with breath held for their Creator's word, counting each second till dawn. What a night is the one that falls on Holy Saturday and yields to the Easter sun! For God is not reanimating our battered old souls, making of us some kind of newer, better Frankenstein. No. God is transforming our every particle, making us into creatures we have never before been.

And so God wakens us to the piercing light of Easter, beings as new as the dawn. All about us, all within us, pulses afresh with new life. We weep at the wonder of it. It is a day of surprise, a day to laugh aloud in delight, a day to catch at our breath.

PRAYERS OF STILLNESS

Into your hands I commend my spirit. Amen.

Lord, it seems the film of my life has frozen on a single frame. I'm stuck and feel it will always be so. I'll live this way the rest of my life. Amen.

Chapter Six

A Resurrection Surprise

If we have been united with him in a death like his, we will
certainly be united with him in a resurrection like his.

—Romans 6:5

Out of his anguish he shall see light.

—Isaiah 53:11

I abandoned and forgot myself,
Laying my face on my Beloved;
All things ceased; I went out from myself,
Leaving my cares
Forgotten among the lilies.

—John of the Cross, *The Dark Night*

For you have died, and your life is hidden with Christ in God.

—Colossians 3:3

With the tears of Good Friday dried to salt on our cheeks, we join a band of sorrowing, faithful women. Down a dusty path toward a sealed and borrowed tomb we shuffle, cradling spices to anoint a cold and battered body. Our hopes died two days ago with his last words; the spices anoint our loss as well. We round the last turn, our eyes downcast against stumbling, and lift our faces to an edifice sealed by suspicion, weighted with sin, and utterly without hope.

But what wildness is this?

Crumpled soldiers snore like sleeping infants; the Roman seal is melted clean away; the disk-shaped stone stands aside like a curtain drawn back on a stage. And the aperture, once yawning black and hollow, pulses with light: a brilliance no tomb can hold. The living beam hones each blade of grass at our feet needle sharp and carves our shadows deep into the earthen path; it is too much light to bear, too much for our tender eyes.

We stumble toward the tomb, drawn by its mystery, drawn like moths toward its unbearable light. Jesus' battered body is gone; in his place sits a pair of mirth-filled angels, full of holy chuckles at our confused awe. Do we hear all round us giggles of heavenly delight?

As on feet winged with wild hope we flee to tell others, for we, too, are resurrected. We shout simply to hear our voices in the bright, open air; we delight in the feel and sound of our sandaled feet against the weathered path; our skin tingles as the rising sun warms the world to new life.

All along we knew death was true and real. But resurrection is truer, realer, still. Death is not the end, but the beginning — the door into adventure.

—ᴠᴠ—

Each day, as I follow Austin's Town Lake trail around its bends and bridges, I come to a place I call "the wood between the worlds." If you have read C. S. Lewis's book *The Magician's Nephew,* you know what I mean. It's a silent, rich, and dreamy sort of place: the kind of wood where you speak quietly and walk just a bit slower. A magic place.

The trees in Austin's wood between the worlds grow right up to the path and stretch toward heaven like arms lifted in adoration. Bushes loaded with greenery grow from a cushion of grasses. During the spring and summer, branches hang heavy with leaves. Greenness fills every space; I walk between solid walls of foliage beneath a canopy of luminous leaves. Bathed in sunlight, they glow like living emeralds. When rain falls, the leaves drink it in with eager lips; I can almost feel them growing.

But come autumn, the leaves turn red or yellow and then brown. They tumble from the trees onto the path; my shoes no longer crunch against the gravel but crackle against their brittle bodies. In time, the leaves decay into a soft, pungent carpet, and then ride the winds of winter and disappear. A chilly sky hovers over bare gray tree branches. I can see far into the woods where only confused tangles of underbrush remain. It looks pretty hopeless.

That's how Jesus' friends felt when he died; it's how we feel in the night. It seemed to them, it seems to us, like everything good is at an end. But when Jesus' followers stood before the tomb that Easter morn long ago, the angels said, "Why do you look for the living among the dead?" (Luke 24:5) And when dawn breaks open our dark-night tomb, we discover we don't belong here any longer, either! *We cannot see what God hopes for us just now; we're walking blind. How, then, can we trust that this torment is not some kind of punishment?*

✠ *Hell's Fire or Heaven's?* ✠

... the genuineness of your faith — being more precious than gold that,
though perishable, is tested by fire....   — 1 Peter 1:7

"Why don't I fit in?"

"Why can't I be more like _____ ."

"What on earth is wrong with me?"

Sound familiar? It does help some to know we are not alone in
asking these questions, but only some, for our uniqueness seems
often more like some nasty trick than a love-sent gift. It certainly
seemed so to me.

A solemn, interior, high-strung soul from childhood, I was
deeply sensitive to others' disapproval and plagued by the most
irrational fears. In addition, I could ask the most absurd questions, a trait my teachers found disconcerting. In response to one
such query, my third-grade teacher replied: "Honestly, I simply
don't know what makes you tick!" Her jibe came as no surprise;
I'd sensed her animosity for months. Still, her remark identified
my longing. I didn't know what made me "tick" either.

Thanks to personality tests administered in my seminary
classes and Elaine Aron's wonderful book *The Highly Sensitive
Person,* I began to feel named and understood, but the childhood
impressions of weakness and worthlessness lingered on. Frankly,
I hated myself much of the time.

I learned to hide my feelings so I could function, but the only
safe place was deep within my soul, where God's love dwelt. But
when someone was curt or cruel to me, that solace scuttled under
the bushel of my own self-loathing. I prayed — how I prayed —
that God would free me of my extreme intuitiveness and of the
sensitivity that drove me to despair each time I was misjudged or
failed to meet my own expectations.

God didn't answer my prayer as I wished. Instead, God answered more deeply and fully than I could conceive, and is answering still.

In the smelters' fire of ministry, a fire in which both criticism and grace burned hot, God initiated my transformation. I began to see that my intuition and sensitivity could be great gifts in ministry. Sensing someone's inner ache, I could pray for his pain or put a loving arm around her shoulder. Knowing how it felt to be judged, I listened with acceptance. Closed and wounded hearts, feeling safe, began to open.

—ᴡᴡ—

One Friday afternoon I was making hospital rounds. It had been a taxing week and I was exhausted. Still, I had one last visit — an elderly woman who had been hospitalized for some time. I stepped into the white and sanitized room where she sat in a wheelchair, staring dully out the door. Her pain was palpable.

"This is more than physical pain," God spoke to my soul.

The woman and I visited a bit about her illness. Sorrow so weighted her words that they dropped from her mouth and clattered against the linoleum floor. Her soul ache matched and exceeded her physical pain. I knew that feeling.

I asked if I might pray with her. She eagerly agreed, and I took her cold and shaking hand in mine. I can't tell you what I prayed, only that when the words ceased, the earnest prayer began.

"Hold on," God told me. "Hold on to her."

So I held her hand and sent her God's comfort and love, as one beloved child to another. My tears flowed, but I didn't care; I wasn't much thinking of myself. How long I knelt by that steel silver chair I can't say, but her grasp grew firmer and warmer throughout.

In time, I opened my eyes and lifted my head. She was look-ing up, her eyes shining, tear tracks anointing her papery cheeks. How she glowed! We said little in parting; I merely smiled and left, overcome with joy.

—⟋⟋⟍—

Long ago, smelters refined precious metals by submitting chunks of mixed ore time and again to cleansing elements: water, oxygen, and fire. They knew that the worthless-looking hunks housed great treasures. Everything impure would wash or burn or evap-orate away, leaving at the heart something precious, something that only grows purer in the flame. There is good stuff — great good stuff — at the heart of us. In the fire we find that out.

In puritan perfectionism, I'd spent years trying rigidly to rid myself of weakness and sin — in essence, to cast aside what God would transform. John of the Cross invited me, instead, to sur-render myself to God's refining flame. But how? The image of a face raced to my mind: a deeply tanned and weathered face, with smoldering eyes and unruly hair, a face well acquainted with hard work and hard times — but — a face 100 percent alive.

Erratic, Impassioned Peter

We think of Peter with a knowing half smile. His rash words and actions smack more of the guy down the street than of holy sainthood. Peter we understand. His passions took him all over the map. He was first to name Jesus as the Christ, then turned right around and lectured Jesus on how the Messiah job ought to work — absolutely no suffering permitted. When Jesus, wear-ing servant garb, approached Peter with a basin of water, the disciple asserted, "You will never wash my feet." When Jesus ex-plained the act's communal significance, Peter demanded, "Lord, not my feet only but also my hands and my head!" We have to love this guy! That same night, he brashly told Jesus, "I will lay down my life for you." A few hours later, in the blackness of fear and night, Peter denied even knowing his Lord — thrice. Easter morn found him diving into the empty tomb (leaving John to stand respectfully outside), but then he turned around and went home. Not knowing what else to do, Peter returned to his former employment.

Standing aboard his fishing boat, Peter spied a man on shore, roasting fish for an early breakfast. Recognizing the beloved visage even from a distance, Peter threw himself into the water. His desire could not abide the ship's slow progress; he swam to his Lord. After breakfast, Jesus gave the impassioned apostle, not a lecture, not a reproof, but a call to deeper love and new work. And Peter, impassioned, forgiven, and challenged, went from that dawn breakfast into a new call. He healed, he stood up to the powers that be ("We cannot keep from speaking about what we have seen and heard," Acts 4:20), he preached with passion. Yet he was still good, old Peter: messing up and starting over, letting fear lead him around by the nose, then remembering his transformation and giving it another go. I find Peter mighty heartening.

When the night baptizes us in fire, it stings. Yet everything we offer to the flame, God transforms. If we hide our flaws and passions in shame or if we flagellate ourselves with guilt, if we insist on fixing ourselves, God's night cannot do its work. The dark night challenges us to release our need to be perfect, and to let God embrace us just as we are. We can spend the rest of our lives weeping with Peter in the night, or, on the dawn of a new day, we can swim ashore and join a resurrected Jesus for a flame-baked breakfast.

For John of the Cross, God was living flame and we the wood. At first, God's flames lick the dust, fungus, and mold that grow outside our bark. Then God's work intensifies, raising the temperature, purging us in flame. In the fire's earnestness, the wood begins to transform. Flames push deep inside us, searching out pockets of resin and whatever filth hides within, purifying us to our very core. Last, the fire transforms the wood until both are one — the wood is unified with the fire. We are unified with God.

John knew the sting of God's fire well, for it burned in him as he languished in a filthy cell.

John's Fiery Trial[21]

If we were to condense John's life story into one word, that word must be love. It began before he was born when, over his family's strong objections, John's father-to-be married the woman he loved. Not many years into the marriage, John's father died, leaving his mother, Catalina, to raise three boys alone. John was just eight years old.

Catalina found no help among her husband's relatives. Soon the middle brother died, leaving the eldest, Francisco, and John, the youngest. Destitute, the family moved to Medina del Campo, where John, now a young teen, attended Jesuit school and worked in a hospital, tending the sick — many from venereal disease. He cared for the forgotten: those left to rot and die alone. Recognizing John's gifts, the hospital director offered him a chaplaincy, a post that would grant his mother some reprieve from her grinding schedule. John struggled with the decision, but finally made his way to the Carmelite monastery and took orders as a monk. John's decision set in motion events that would lead to physical and spiritual torment.

John yearned for a more primitive order where, in solitude, he could more clearly listen to and serve his Lord. As he considered his options, John met a woman who changed the direction of his life — a capable, strong prioress named Teresa of Avila. Teresa was reforming the Carmelite nuns — hoping to return the order to its earlier, simpler life — and she invited John to do the same for the Carmelite monks. He agreed. His first monastery, established with the help of two other dedicated brothers, was stark indeed: little more in the beginning than a dirty barn. Yet doing God's work and living simply gave John incredible joy.

However, politics soon intruded into John's simple world. The older *calced* (with shoes) order grew wary of Teresa and John's new *discalced* (without shoes) "rival faction." Already over fifty nuns had been excommunicated for choosing Teresa as their prioress. Then, as John traveled the Spanish landscape, caring for the sick and counseling those in need, the clash of the rival orders caught up with him. One night, calced monks and soldiers abducted John from his hut outside the city of Avila. During morning mass, John escaped, racing back across the frozen landscape to his hut where he destroyed documents of the reform. He finished the job just as his captors reappeared.

They marched him along a circuitous route to Toledo, avoiding towns where the small monk might be recognized. In Toledo, the abductors cast John into a closet cell near the monastery toilets: a windowless space barely ten feet by six feet across. He had only two coarse blankets and some boards as bedding and a pail to serve as his toilet. The cell's only light came from a space high in the wall scarcely two feet across. By climbing onto a support, holding his book at just the right angle, and straining his eyes, John could read his daily devotions. Here, John would face his greatest torment.

Months of incarceration and abuse, punctuated by a demeaning weekly ritual, devitalized John's physical and mental health: "Every week on Fridays Fray Juan was dragged to the common dining room where he was given bread and water — his sole sustenance for that day. As the other monks ate their food on tables located around the walls of the large refectory, Fray Juan ate his bread kneeling on the hard, stone floor in the very center of the room. Once finished, the superior would begin to harangue him in the presence of all the others:

"'You, Juan de la Cruz, are but a rebellious, stubborn man who desires nothing but your own fame and honor.... How can you maintain your satanic stance in the face of such horrors you are causing? Repent of your disobedience.'"[22]

When the superior finished his tirade, the monks filed by John, chanting. With a knotted rope, each brother, in turn, whipped the prisoner. Bloodied and starving, John was then returned to his filthy cell.

Worse yet, as he lay in his cell, wounded and aching, doubts chafed at his heart. Perhaps he was wrong. Perhaps he was not serving his Lord. Perhaps he deserved what he was getting. And then, to fuel the torment, sinful passions besieged him. He was visited by temptations he thought long ago squelched.

The rival monks fed him propaganda: his order had collapsed, everyone else had given up, all was lost. Yet the greatest agony came not from his abductors, but from his Lord. In the filthy, dark Toledo cell, John lost all sense of God's presence. Despair crushed the monk's body, mind, and spirit. He had no one in whom to confide his torment. John wanted to die.

In time the anguish lessened; even in the dark cell, day was dawning. John began to compose poetry, escaping for a time from his confines into the beauty of God's love and creation.

Later he was to compose a poem and commentary of hope about this, his darkest night.

Nine months passed; John grew more and more frail. If he did not escape, he would die in prison. Each day, John loosened the latch on his cell door until one night when he pushed the latch free; it clattered against the floor, and he listened breathlessly as disturbed sleepers wondered at the noise. When they did not rise, John slipped from his cell, and, with a rope made from his blankets, climbed down the prison wall, and jumped onto the stone roof below. The ailing monk then threaded his way through Toledo's dark streets toward a convent of sympathetic, discalced nuns. (This is one account of John's escape. Others exist.)

John recovered and went right back to work, demonstrating a wisdom and gentleness that drew people to him. He traveled widely, ministering as he went, caring for the poor. And he wrote a commentary on his prison poem, "The Dark Night." In the commentary, John described God's purging, transformative fire.

In his late forties, wounds he had contracted in prison festered into an ankle ulcer. More ulcers appeared, traveling up his leg. John had contracted *erysipelas*. He would die slowly and in great pain.

Near midnight on December 13, 1591, John asked to hear the Scriptures that had nurtured his lifelong faith, passages burning with passion and rife with images of God's seeking love: the Song of Songs: "As they were read, he kept repeating: 'What marvelous pearls! What marvelous pearls....' The bell rang for Matins. Fray Juan asked, 'What was that?' 'The bell calling the brothers to Matins,' they answered. 'Glory to God. I shall say them in heaven,' he replied, looking at each one as if giving them a personal message. Once more he kissed the cross, closed his eyes

and said, 'In manus tuas, Domine, commendo spiritum meum' "
[Into your hands, Lord, I commend my spirit.][23]

A soul afire with love for God entered heaven that day, a soul
purged in the blessed burnings of the night.

Over the years, God has used both pain and joy as a refining fire, purifying everything in my soul that I will submit to
the flame. What God's fire touches, it transforms. To be swept
into God's furnace is to know — to begin knowing — all I've a
potential to be.

I still struggle with self-acceptance, still resist God's transforming fire. But when I recall the last words of a tiny monk, the
preaching of an erratic fisherman, and an aged woman's face upturned to God, I am grateful beyond grateful to be who I am.
We are, indeed, designed with love. *We have been swept into God's
furnace, and we have stayed put. Will the purging never end?*

PRAYERS IN THE FLAME

*Are the fires of hell and those of heaven one and the same, God? They
feel it just now. Amen.*

Have mercy. Amen.

LIFELINES

Search for Nothing by Richard P. Hardy: In this biography of
John of the Cross, we discover the humanity and humor of
the man who gave name to the "dark night."

The Voyage of the Dawn Treader by C. S. Lewis: Boasting one of
the best opening book lines ever, Lewis lets us first despise "that
record stinker, Eustace" (p. 5) and then chuckle at his foolishness,
imagine his torment, and finally marvel at the transformation of his
selfish soul.

Ordinary People directed by Robert Redford: In a family tested by fire, some emerge purged while others are consumed. What are trials making of us?

Regarding Henry directed by Mike Nichols: Why is this movie so overlooked? Henry Turner (Harrison Ford), in forgetting what seems most important, remembers what really counts. I want to put my arms around this film.

It's a Wonderful Life directed by Frank Capra: Trial by fire, Christmas — oh, and Jimmy Stewart. Enough said.

"He's Alive!" by Don Francisco: The ballad of Peter's agony, it's the real stuff of Easter.

"Revival" by Robin Mark: Mark responds to widespread violence in his Irish homeland with toe-tapping praise music. When he belts out "Revive us with your fire!" we can't keep from singing.

The Ecstasy of St. Teresa by Bernini: Teresa of Avila described a vision in which God's angel pieced her heart with a fiery arrow. Bernini created an anything but staid sculpture of the moment. Nothing prudish here!

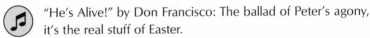

✠ *Is It Over?* ✠

You guide me with your counsel, and afterward you will receive me with honor. — Psalm 73:24

A writers' conference speaker once remarked, "I prefer saying 'I have writ' to 'I am writing.'" I know the feeling. Writing can be grueling work; wordsmiths like having it done. Just so with the dark night: at dawn, it's a delight to look back on where the darkness has led me. I'd like to think I'm finished now, that I can delight in an Easter glow the rest of my life. But I know better.

Yes, I have opened my hands a bit and let go some idols, I have endured the sense of God's abandonment and employed spiritual practices to remain connected, I have ridden God's raging ocean and stayed put in God's purging fire. As a result, I greet Easter's dawn lighter and freer. And I think that's quite good enough — well, better, at least.

Faced with the prospect of another night, I respond: "I'm just about as liberated as I'd like, thanks anyway. Let's just leave well enough alone." Frankly, I prefer the known — even if it's constrictive. And in this I am not alone. Victor Frankl's book *Man's Search for Meaning* recounts his liberation from the Nazi concentration camp after years of internment. He and his fellow prisoners wandered away from camp during the day, but by nightfall they all returned to the very place of their imprisonment. "In the evening when we all met again in our hut, one said secretly to the other, 'Tell me, were you pleased today?'

"And the other replied, feeling ashamed as he did not know that we all felt similarly, 'Truthfully, no!' "[24]

Frankl and his friends had lived so long as prisoners, that incarceration had become their norm. Freedom felt like fear.

We are not yet as free as God would have us be, which means more invitations to let go, more purging flames. If we have courage enough, if we have passion enough, we will stand, again, on the edge of night.

The night's cycle of suffering, death, and resurrection will continue throughout our lifetime. Still, we needn't be so fearful next time around, for we've learned much from this journey. We recognize that our only task is to endure, we have explored spiritual practices to help us hold on, we've seen one night end in brilliant morn. We can, at last, acknowledge the night as God's mysterious blessing.

The cycle will continue until *the* adventure — the great one — calls our name. Perhaps we won't embark on this adventure for decades or perhaps the venture further up and further in calls to us now. Humanity's boldest adventure bursts through all knowledge owned by those called "the living" and answers, for eternity, the questions of the night. *We see in nature, in the story of Christ's passion, in the journey of the night, a cycle that goes on until our death. Can we know, really know, what waits on the other side?*

CYCLICAL PRAYERS

I celebrate the night, God, but not enough to do it again. Help me. Amen.

It's the known I trust, God. Help me trust you even more. Amen.

Where is all this going, God? I'm afraid. Amen.

LIFELINES

Man's Search for Meaning by Victor Frankl: Are we ready for post-night freedom? Frankl had the courage to transform his dark agony into a gift. And it's still giving.

Everything Belongs by Richard Rohr: Rohr invites me to move in deeper, to recognize that everything — broken, wounded, raging me included — belongs to God. Published as a work on contemplative prayer, it's really a call to contemplative living. It's a deep and wide book: one I'll spend my lifetime contemplating.

Wild Strawberries directed by Ingmar Bergman: Slow paced and acted as an understatement that makes it agonizingly real, the movie wonders at God's existence as it chronicles the life of an aging man who once thought himself good. His life choices play out cyclically in the next generation and threaten the one yet to come.

"Tallis Canon" or "All Praise to You, My God, This Night" by Thomas Ken and Thomas Tallis: Hum it, sing it as a round, or sit back in the dark and just listen. Might this darkness truly be the shelter of God's wings?

"Day by Day" by Stephen Schwartz: From the musical *Godspell,* "Day By Day" prays a prayer that keeps us enduring night by night.

Isenheim Altarpiece by Mathias Grünewald: When the wings are closed, Christ's scars and dying hands say it all: Good Friday is unbearable. When the wings are opened, the risen Christ, clothed in the sunrise, knocks soldiers clean off their pins. Now that's Easter!

✠ *Toward Home* ✠

Jesus' resurrection—the first fruit of our own transformation—is history's most stunning story. Yet the resurrection of Jesus bespeaks a miracle that God worked into creation from the very beginning. Across time and from every corner of God's creation, resurrection shouts its joy. Dead winter bulbs bloom into spring tulips; great-grandfather's chin appears again in the face of our newborn; from the ashes of despair a phoenix rises: glorious, new, unexpected.

The phoenix, a creature who inhabits one world and, in the same moment, the next...

RESURRECTION PRAYERS

Thanks to you, Lord, I am the phoenix. Kill me again and again and raise me to new life until the day I shed forever this body of death and live with you in utter freedom. Amen.

I am a valley of dry bones, Lord. Dead to the present, lost in the agony of the past. You alone can breathe me alive. O Lord, either scatter my bones to the forgetting winds or breathe on me and make me live anew. Amen.

Set my soul afire, Lord. Transform all into your image. Amen.

CHAPTER SEVEN

FURTHER UP AND FURTHER IN

But rejoice insofar as you are sharing Christ's sufferings, so that you may also be glad and shout for joy when his glory is revealed.

— 1 Peter 4:13

Even though our outer nature is wasting away, our inner nature is being renewed day by day. For this slight momentary affliction is preparing us for an eternal weight of glory beyond all measure, because we look not at what can be seen but at what cannot be seen; for what can be seen is temporary, but what cannot be seen is eternal.

— 2 Corinthians 4:16–18

He turned swiftly round, crouched lower, lashed himself with his tail and shot away like a golden arrow. "Come further in! Come further up!" he shouted over his shoulder.

— C. S. Lewis, *The Last Battle*

When he is revealed, we will be like him, for we will see him as he is.

— 1 John 3:2

Did you do it as a child — feign sleep on Christmas Eve night, then slip downstairs to peek through a keyhole at the magic of a coming Christmas? I did. I remember the feel of chilly floor beneath my bare feet as I crept down the hall, the cozy warmth of my flannel pajamas, and the tree, dark in its midnight corner but glistening all over with gems of colored light. I recall what seemed to me mountains of gifts, their foil wrappings catching the gleam of Christmas lights and giving silent promise of tomorrow's joy.

The greatest of holidays awaits us once we leap free of our flesh and all its limits. We think we know nothing of that mystery world, but perhaps God permits us from time to time a glimpse through the keyhole. It may happen as we walk at dusk or when we listen to great music. It may happen as we read scripture, paint a picture, or even as we sit in traffic. It may occur during prayer — suddenly we have no need for words or images. Time evaporates, and we have no thought of ourself as a separate self. In that moment outside time, we are fully whole — beyond the limitations of body, time, and space — at one with God.

In this, the unitive experience, we peek through the keyhole and receive a foretaste of heaven. Our hearts beat with God's heart and all is perfectly well. George MacDonald, author of *Phantasies, The Princess and the Goblin,* and *Lilith,* describes its inexplicable quality thus: "It is but that the deeper soul that willed and wills our souls, rises up, the infinite Life, into the Self we call *I* and *me,* makes the *I* and *me* more and more his, and himself more and more ours; until at length the glory of our existence flashes upon us ... we are one with God for ever and ever."[25]

What, then, awaits us after death? What is this blessed union toward which the dark night draws us? What is the whole scene that we can only glimpse darkly through life's keyhole? When I ask these questions, I think of Joyce.

And I think of Uncle Paul.

✠ *How Are the Kids?* ✠

Seek the things that are above, where Christ is, seated at the right hand of God.   — Colossians 3:1

A slender woman, she had flashing red hair: long hair that curled around her shoulders and framed her face like a Titian halo. No room could quite contain the force of her personality. Nor her voice. Joyce, in her mezzo soprano voice, could belt out Southern gospel and have the people next door dancing around their furniture. She was young and beautiful, a loving wife and an exuberant mother. And she was dying.

I don't know the pain of watching a spouse die, but I know what it is to see my brother watch his wife waste away. Of course we all prayed. Of course we all hoped. Surely God would spare her — for the sake of her children, for the sake of her vivacious witness.

I didn't know her well. We only saw one another on holidays, and whereas she was the shimmering day illuminating any room in which she stood, drawing people to her like a magnet, I was the silent night, content in my small corner, mirroring the emotions of whomever drew near. When I learned that she had advanced cancer, it seemed an obscenity. She still glowed with health and energy.

Even when she said, "That chemo is going to kick my butt," it was with the half grin of someone born to win. And fight to win she did: surgeries, chemo, radiation, emergency room visits, more surgeries month after month after month.

Far away on my prayer walks, I took her daily into my heart, tried to carry some of the pain, implored God to fill her body with healing light. And I felt her presence on those walks, as if she knew what I was about.

Near the end, I flew up to Arkansas. My parents, faithful to her care and that of the children, met me at the airport and drove me to the hospital. Mainly, I sat in the background and marveled at my brother—the nemesis of my childhood days—as he reeled off medical information to the nurse and pluckily stood up for his wife's needs when hospital policy didn't fit them. He was respectful, but he was determined.

I spoke with her only briefly on leaving.

"Will you come back?" she asked.

"I will."

"When?"

"In two weeks. I'll see you then."

"I love you."

"I love you, Joyce."

She died before I returned, just a few days after her thirty-eighth birthday. But that last visit—I can see her still. She was so thin, so frail; the power and light of God shone right through her.

After her death, a blankness descended on my prayer walks. I could not feel her spirit — nor God's either. Where was she? Where was God? Months, dull months, rolled by. By sheer determination, I plodded through the fury of summer programming. My heart ached for my brother, who had stood in the pulpit at Joyce's funeral and said with tears in his eyes, "You were never a burden." I ached for Jordan and Colten, growing up without hugs from their joyous, courageous mother. Who can measure such a loss? It seemed a crime against nature.

"I hadn't planned on raising these kids alone," my brother had said. Yet he was, and doing the best he could. Still, I felt from him and from the children that something was amiss. They laughed, we played, but I felt an ache in them. And one in myself. I needed to know all was well with Joyce. I knew what Jesus said about eternity, and I believed it. But any sense of her spirit was completely snuffed out to my perception.

Jung wrote of the wisdom of the unconscious. One night I had a dream. In it, our whole family attended a singing service in a small stone church like the one in which I'd been baptized. We sang the grand old hymns that got your feet tapping — the kind Joyce loved to sing. After the service, we met together in an alcove behind the baptistery. There was Joyce, sitting on a gleaming hospital gurney, shining with life and health!

"How are your girls?" she asked me, just as she'd always done and as if nothing extraordinary had happened at all.

Someone tried to tell her she'd died, but it didn't take — like water off a duck's back, as my dad would say. To her the words didn't matter, as if they were a kind of gobbledygook from some other reality.

When I awoke, I had an assurance that Joyce — the irrepressible, shining, red-headed spirit that made her Joyce — was quite well. Shortly after the dream, my dad telephoned to say that, though still grieving, my brother and the kids had turned a corner. He thought they were going to make it through all right.

I shared the dream with a friend. "It was like she knew something we didn't," I puzzled.

And because my friend is wise, she responded, "Let's hope we all know more after we've died."

And lived.

When I think of eternity, I think of Joyce. Of how I hope that, in whatever form our resurrected selves take, we'll still be able to smile and ask about the kids. That we'll enjoy a good toe-tapping gospel song and be so very well that the aches of this world no longer make any sense. *Dreaming has its wisdom, but is it wise to give up so much in this life with no tangible assurance that anything comes after?*

Prayers for the Dying and Dead

Love them in death, gracious God, as you loved them in life. Amen.

Is there really any point in praying for the dead? It doesn't really matter, Lord, because we cannot help but pray. Amen.

LIFELINES

Lilith by George MacDonald: George MacDonald, bless him, is a ponderous writer. I must force myself through the initial chapters of his book, but then the power of his myth making takes over. Lilith is dark, troubling, sensuous, and obscure — like my mind much of the time, especially in the night!

A Ring of Endless Light by Madeleine L'Engle: A book about teens, it's too good to miss at any age. *Endless Light* is raw and real and tormenting — but its hope is just as real as its suffering. A favorite.

What Dreams May Come directed by Vincent Ward: Death is not only powerless to sever loving relationships, death might even bring them to a deeper level. Think on the possibilities....

Contact directed by Robert Zemeckis: Need permission to color outside the lines and think *sans* box? *Contact* transcends not only galaxies, but death as well. Soul expanding stuff.

"Graverobber" by Petra: This is my idea of funeral music! It's gospel: clean, raw, and pulsing with hope.

"Finale" from *Les Misérables* by Alain Boublil and Claude-Michael Schönberg: What is a good death? This song helps us know.

The *Burial of Count Orgaz* by El Greco: While St. Stephen and St. Augustine lay the faithful count to rest, a welcoming committee awaits in heaven. El Greco paints two realities into one picture and thus gives hope to the dying. Who will come round to welcome *us* home?

✠ *Are We There Yet?* ✠

In my Father's house there are many dwelling places. If it were not so, would I have told you that I go to prepare a place for you?

—John 14:2

In my earliest memories, he's fishing: hat jammed down over those protuberant taxicab ears, tongue wedged into his jaw, intense concentration in those clear eyes. It was the natural order of things; at each visit we'd amble down to the pond, he toting his rod and reel, me shouldering a borrowed cane pole. Sometimes others would come along, oftimes it was just we two. We'd spend hours casting, waiting, casting again, watching ripples shimmer out and out all the way to pond's edge, tasting life's goodness. I noticed nothing different about Paul except that he still lived in Grandma and Grandpa's farmhouse though my dad had left years before to marry and raise a family.

"Why don't ya get married? Don't ya wanna get married?" I endlessly pestered.

Always I'd get the same answer, Missouri slow and unperturbed, "Ah, I don't need to get married."

Where or when Dad told that me that Paul had mental retardation, I don't recall; I just remember it didn't matter. He was my best fishing buddy (he'd hook worms for me when I felt too squeamish to do it myself), he always shared his gadgets (including Hairy Harry, the metal shavings man), and I loved him.

One Sunday morning just barely into my double-digit years, I perched on a worn wooden pew inside Pleasant Hill Baptist Church and first glimpsed Uncle Paul's faith. Invited by the pastor to share favorite Scripture verses, person after person stood and read. Paul's hand slowly rose. He stood, one hand in his Sunday-morning overalls pocket, the other cradling his worn Bible. Without faltering and almost from memory, he read: "For I am persuaded, that neither death, nor life, nor angels, nor principalities, nor powers, nor things present, nor things to come. Nor height, nor depth, nor any other creature, shall be able to separate us from the love of God, which is in Christ Jesus our Lord" (Romans 8:38–39 KJV).

The sanctuary fell silent. Uncle Paul sat down, closed his Bible, and bowed his head. As morning light anointed his freshly washed and carefully parted hair, he seemed to me almost too fine to touch. I stared, awed. Paul had read and drawn meaning from this deep, wide, soaring passage: it was his favorite.

When Grandma died years later, Grandpa and Paul moved from their farm to a nursing home. When we journeyed across the miles to visit their small, shared room, Grandpa would jump up, arms outstretched, but Paul we couldn't predict. Sometimes he'd be happy to see us and delighted with the gifts we brought — sometimes clearly not! Uncle Paul was incapable of pretense; he was, quite simply, just what he seemed.

Years passed; I married, moved away, and rarely saw my favorite uncle. One night, my dad's voice, pressed hollow through miles of phone line, relayed news of Grandpa's death. How would Paul cope? He'd never faced a world without Grandpa; would the loss shatter Paul's small world?

"The Lord and I will get through this together," he told concerned friends and relatives. And they did. Paul stayed at the nursing home, where he played checkers, listened to his radio, and meticulously completed every paint-by-number piece that came his way (I'm privileged to own two of Paul's paintings).

He lived into his seventies, but at last, energy and strength ebbed; Paul was wearing old.

Two years ago Uncle Paul died. Weary with suffering, he yearned to "just go home." I have no doubt — none whatever — that Uncle Paul is, this moment, with God. I cannot but imagine my uncle in freshly washed, cotton-comfortable overalls, playing one feisty game of heavenly checkers.

And I believe he's right at home, that he looks frankly into the eyes of his beloved Jesus and that Jesus' eyes twinkle merrily in return. No awkward pauses mar their conversation; no misinterpretations in meaning or intent hamper the visit. Jesus and Uncle Paul visit just like old friends — because that's what they are. Paul finds in heaven all the comforts of home because he spent his life making friends with the owner and growing to like the accommodations.

All his life, Uncle Paul believed God mattered more than anything else. Paul's faith was utterly childlike and thus profoundly wise. He simply loved God with all his heart.

Believers have, across the centuries, depicted heaven with wondrous metaphors: a golden, glittering city; the real world, of which ours is merely a shadow; the realization of our most profound dreams. It's marvelous to imagine.

Yet the most wondrous, breathtaking gift of heaven will be God's welcoming presence. Let us, like Uncle Paul, love God with all our hearts so we may drink deep of heaven throughout all eternity.

Aslan invites, "Come further in! Come further up!"

Julian of Norwich assures, "All shall be well."

Jesus promises, "I have gone to prepare a place for you."

The road home leads sometimes through a dark night. Yes, we feel lonely — but we are not alone. Yes, it seems we are standing still — but God is drawing us safely home. Let us be guided ever onward by God's abiding love. And let us find when we arrive a warm light in the window, a wide-open door, and Jesus' face, alight with eager welcome.

I thank God for giving me the night that I might know even more deeply the love that draws me homeward. It will be enough — indeed, far more than enough — if my Lord and brother takes my face between his hands and, with eyes brimming full of loving pride, says: "Well done, faithful servant. Well done, cherished sister. I'm so glad to have you home at last."

Until then, Peace be unto you, and hope. And love, God's love, especially this. Amen.

PRAYERS AT THE PORTAL

Lord and brother, you are my dearest friend. I want to run headlong past death's portals and into your open arms. Tell me then — tell me now — that all is eternally well. Amen.

You who loved us in life, love us now as we cross this new sea. Amen.

LIFELINES

The Last Battle by C. S. Lewis: I love all the Narnia Chronicles, but I find the first (*The Lion, the Witch, and the Wardrobe*) and last the most potent. In *Battle*...Aslan bids us take the eternal adventure "further up and further in!" My heart races at the prospect.

"The Crossing of the Bar" by Alfred Lord Tennyson: As death neared, Tennyson requested that this small poem conclude all compilations of his published poetry. Just read it — out loud — you'll understand.

The Seventh Seal directed by Ingmar Bergman: Set during the Crusades and the Black plague, Bergman's brilliant, intense film probes death and dying from myriad perspectives. The scene in the confessional asks the questions of the night. Watch it at least twice!

"Amazing Grace" by John Newton: It's the beloved hymn everyone knows. In my opinion, we should do the "Hallelujah Chorus" standing thing when we sing its last stanza.

"Don't Pay the Ferryman" by Chris de Burgh: Not his best-selling song, but in my opinion his best. Rife with images from Greek myth, "Ferryman" suggests that dying well might be about living well.

The Starry Night by Vincent van Gogh: In van Gogh's time, people believed that, after death, we found a home in the stars. Perhaps Vincent had such hope when he looked out the window of his mental asylum and painted such magic.

⊙otes

1. C. S. Lewis, *A Grief Observed* (New York: The Seabury Press, 1961), 9.

2. Ibid., 38.

3. Ibid., 54–55.

4. *Parzival.* Retold by Katherine Paterson (New York: Puffin Books, 1998), 100–101.

5. Ibid., 122.

6. C. S. Lewis, *The Silver Chair* (New York: HarperCollins, 1980), 27.

7. J. R. R. Tolkein, *The Return of the King* (Boston: Houghton Mifflin Co., 1987), 195.

8. Henri Nouwen, *A Cry for Mercy.* Rueben P. Job and Norman Shawchuck, *A Guide to Prayer for Ministers and Other Servants* (Nashville: The Upper Room, 1983), 288.

9. Dorothy C. Bass, ed., *Practicing Our Faith* (San Francisco: Jossey-Bass Publishers, 1997); Joan Chittister, OSB, *Wisdom Distilled from the Daily* (San Francisco: HarperSanFrancisco, 1990).

10. We cannot begin to address the issue of depression in these few sentences. See Appendix B for additional resources.

11. "A Night of Surrender" and "A Sacred Suffering" explore the first shade of night — the Night of the Senses — and introduce the deepest shade of night: the Night of the Spirit.

12. St. John of the Cross, *Dark Night of the Soul,* trans. Mirabai Starr (New York: Riverhead Books, 2002), 58.

13. Ibid., 118.

14. Julian of Norwich, *The Revelation of Divine Love in Sixteen Showings,* trans. M. L. del Mastro (Liguori, MO: Liguori/Triumph, Liguori, 1977), 102.

15. *www.appleseeds.org/god-speak.htm.*

16. Simone Weil, *Waiting on God,* trans. Emma Craufurd (New York: Harper Perennial Classics, 2001), 70.

17. The story of Therese of Lisieux's life is based on: Therese of Lisieux, *Autobiography of St. Therese of Lisieux,* trans. Ronald Knox (New York: P. J. Kenedy & Sons, 1958), Therese of Lisieux: Story of a Life: *therese.kashalinka .com/biography/biog_11.shtml,* and Catholic Online: *www.catholic.org/saints/ saint.php?saint/_id=105.*

18. Ibid., 254.

19. Ibid., 255–56.

20. Ibid., 312.

21. The story of John of the Cross's life is based on: Richard P. Hardy, *Search for Nothing: The Life of John of the Cross* (New York: Crossroad, 1982) and Gerald May, *The Dark Night of the Soul: A Psychiatrist Explores the Connection between Darkness and Spiritual Growth* (San Francisco: HarperSanFrancisco, 2004).

22. Hardy, *Search for Nothing,* 67–68.

23. Ibid., 111.

24. Victor Frankl, *Man's Search for Meaning* (New York: Washington Square Press, 1984), 110.

25. George MacDonald, *Creation in Christ,* ed. Rueben P. Job and Norman Shawchuck, *A Guide to Prayer for Ministers and Other Servants* (Nashville: The Upper Room, 1983), 267.

26. *Dark Night of the Soul,* 160.

27. Ibid., 161.

28. Ibid., 161–68.

Appendix A

What Is
Spiritual Direction?

Who will hope for us when we are without hope? A spiritual director listens with us for the Holy Spirit's gentle breath. A director does not provide answers; she accompanies our faith journey, pointing out evidences of God's work along the way, assuring us in the dark times that God does love us and that all will be well.

Spiritual direction differs in purpose from therapy. Whereas a therapist's intent is psychological and curative, a spiritual director focuses on listening to the Spirit and accompanying the directee's spiritual journey. Spiritual direction is holy attentiveness. A spiritual direction session may consist of discussion between a director and a directee, or of silent, listening prayer. A good director follows the Spirit and the directee's lead, perhaps suggesting a spiritual practice to try on for size, perhaps recommending a helpful resource. Spiritual direction nurtures our connection with God and challenges our growth.

We often seek spiritual direction from friends or parents, but God has gifted some people in the art of listening who have gone on to receive training to sharpen and enhance their skills. Though they carry the title spiritual director, spiritual companion or one who listens in hope might better describe their function.

Why not simply rely on friends and relatives in the dark night? Quite simply because in the night, our souls are raw and laid bare. Sometimes, with the best of intentions, people say wounding things. A spiritual director is trained to be safe and supportive.

We find a spiritual director by consulting a minister, who may be a trained director or can refer us to one, or by contacting a Catholic or Episcopal church for a referral. Catholics and Episcopalians have been doing spiritual direction for centuries and are, therefore, fine resources. The books and Web site below offer additional possibilities.

Once we find a prospective spiritual director, we conduct a brief fact-finding telephone conversation with him or her. Some important topics to address include the following:

1. How the referral was made

2. The director's spiritual calling and technique (Why do you do spiritual direction? How do you understand your role as a spiritual director?)

3. Our need and intent ("I think I might be in a dark night. What resources might you have for seeing me through this time?")

4. Monetary considerations. What, if anything, does the spiritual director charge, and how does he or she prefer to be paid?

We then schedule a discernment appointment so we can visit face to face with the spiritual director. After the appointment we assess our response with questions like: "Can I grow to trust this person? Did the session focus primarily on my relationship with God? Did the director feel a need to prove him or herself? Was his or her focus on listening to me or on 'fixing' the problem?

Do I respect the director's faith? Will my faith be both respected and challenged? Do I feel hopeful about what might come out of the relationship?"

If the first spiritual director we consult is not a good match, we need feel no guilt in seeking another. A good spiritual director will understand and support such a choice.

Good Reads

Edwards, Tilden. *Spiritual Director/Spiritual Companion.* A serene, informative book by a leader in the field; even the book is Spirit filled.

Guenther, Margaret. *Holy Listening: The Art of Spiritual Direction.* Guenther sprinkles her text with wonderful stories. Gentle and womanly, *Holy Listening* depicts spiritual direction as nurture.

Kelsey, Morton. *Companions on the Inner Way.* Accessibly written and explicated with graphs for the visual learner, Kelsey celebrates the mystical and urges the reader to work with a director who is, herself, on a journey.

Leech, Kenneth. *Soul Friend.* Densely written and replete with quotes from every imaginable field of study, Leech grounds spiritual direction throughout history and in today's world.

May, Gerald. *Care of Mind: Care of Spirit.* In this intelligent book, May clarifies the difference between spiritual direction and psychotherapy as well as the need for both.

Good Web Site

www.sdiworld.org

Appendix B

Finding a Therapist

You awake in the morning dreading the day — and it's not the first time. You've little patience with yourself and with others. The world feels gray, hopeless, worthless, pointless.

We all go through seasons of the blues, but ongoing depression requires treatment. Although some faith systems insist that the choice to seek treatment equals lack of faith in God, the opposite is actually true. The courage to look at our brokenness, believing God loves us as we are, is an act of enormous faith.

A personal referral is most apt to result in a good match for us. Listed below, in order of my preference, are some resources for finding a therapist.

+ Ministers who know us and can recommend therapists
+ Friends who work in the field of psychology and/or have access to therapists
+ Friends from other congregations who can consult their ministers for referrals (if our congregation proves unsupportive)
+ Physicians
+ Phone directories under Psychologist, Marriage and Family Therapist, or Psychiatrist (psychiatrists are physicians who can dispense medication and can often be found under "Physicians")

After selecting two or three possibilities, we make short fact-finding phone calls, addressing some topics like the following:

1. How the referral was made

2. Our therapeutic need and a request for the therapist's credentials ("I think I may be depressed. How might you deal with this?")

3. The therapist's attitude toward faith ("I am a Christian. How would my faith affect your attitude toward me and our work together?")

4. Monetary information, such as the charge per session and insurance coverage

Following an assessment appointment, we ask ourselves, "Is the therapist someone I can learn to trust? Can I be honest with him or her? Can we work together on my healing? If I feel misunderstood, do I feel comfortable correcting him or her? Do I feel hopeful about what might come out of the relationship?"

Then we muster our courage, ask God's help, and begin, remembering that the hard, worthy work of therapy is simply one avenue toward healing. For in the end, it is God who heals.

Good Reads

Friedman, Edwin H. *Friedman's Fables.* Friedman, a rabbi and family therapist, employs stories to open our eyes to our own story — and our own stuff.

May, Gerald. *Addiction and Grace.* We can be addicted to anything. This book invites us to own, then release, our addictive tendencies through trust in God's grace.

May, Gerald. *The Dark Night of the Soul: A Psychiatrist Explores the Connection between Darkness and Spiritual Growth.* A leading psychotherapist explores the purpose of the night and various ways persons experience it.

Good Web Sites

www.depressionscreening.org
www.mentalhealthscreening.org
www.med.nyu.edu/psych/screens/depres.html
www.healthyplace.com/communities/depression/definition.asp

Appendix C

John's Ladder

> It [contemplation] is an infused knowledge of God that both illumines and impassions the soul, drawing her upward step by step into the arms of the Beloved. The ladder of love is so secret that God alone can measure it.[26]

In Chapters 19 and 20 of his commentary on the dark night of the soul, John likens the dark night's journey to a "mystical ladder of divine love."[27] God invites those who desire deeper relationship onto this ladder. John of the Cross believed most Christians take their initial steps onto the ladder as physical death approaches, while God's leading and/or life experiences propel others toward the ladder earlier.

John's ladder takes us through the dark night of the soul from first dusk to full after-death union with God. I offer two cautions before we climb onto John's metaphorical ladder. First, most Westerners are bathed in a competitive spirit along with the amniotic fluid: a success-oriented Western culture shapes our thinking in ways we don't realize. We'll need to wash off our competitive culture — as much as we can — to receive John's teachings as intended. We miss his point if we determine to hustle up the ladder ahead of old so-and-so.

My second disclaimer concerns linear thinking. A ladder helps us conceptualize the dark night journey, but it has its limits. We visualize ourselves straining up the ladder to reach the top, where we can lean back on a heavenly cloud and breathe: "There, now. Made it." During our earthly journey, most of us cycle through many nights and dawns.

So let's hold two additional images in mind as we explore John's ladder. First, imagine the dark night as a vortex within God's very heart: caught in a force beyond our control, fight as we might against its surging, we know in the end that we are helpless. We don't like feeling helpless; we don't like feeling caught in God's sovereignty. Yet our best option is simply to trust ourselves to the wind. The exciting thing about the ride is that, although we touch the same truths in one night and then in another, we move each time through the night's wake with deeper understanding. Our wild journey will not end until death, yet we can learn to taste the wind with growing anticipation.

Taken another way, the dark night journey is like the Christian calendar. During each cycle, we visit Advent, Christmas, Epiphany, Lent, Easter, and Pentecost. We never arrive at Easter without first cycling through Good Friday and Holy Saturday. Each calendar year, if we remain faithful, we can honor Good Friday and Easter Sunday as different people — as deeper people.

Now let's look at John's ladder. He understands the journeyer's ups and downs not as backsliding, but as movement toward soul quietude amidst changing circumstance. Remember playing "Chutes and Ladders" as a child? If we played long enough, we reached the goal. Despite circumstances that send us plummeting down a chute, our overall direction in life is Godward. On John's ladder we will, in time, arrive.

John's Ladder Rung-by-Rung[28]

The chart below depicts each step on John's ladder, a biblical example that helps define the step, and a Scripture that expresses it. Most of the images come from John's commentary (John loved scripture, especially the Song of Songs). As a mystic, John understood the soul — his included — to be feminine, thus the marriage motif. My additions to John's work are marked with asterisks. Following the chart is an explanation of each step.

Step	Biblical Example	Bible Verse
1	Bride in Song of Solomon	Answer me quickly, O LORD; my spirit fails. Psalm 143:7
2	Mary Magdalene at the Tomb	Seek the LORD and his strength; seek his presence continually. Psalm 105:4
3	Jacob's Love for Rachel	I would rather be a doorkeeper in the house of my God than live in the tents of wickedness. Psalm 84:10b*
4	Peter Swimming to Jesus*	Set me as a seal upon your heart, as a seal upon your arm; for love is strong as death, passion fierce as the grave. Song of Solomon 8:6
5	Rachel Longing for a Child	My soul longs, indeed it faints for the courts of the LORD; my heart and my flesh sing for joy to the living God. Psalm 84:2
6	Isaiah's Eagle Prophecy	As a deer longs for flowing streams, so my soul longs for you, O God. Psalm 42:1
7	Moses' Intercession for Israel	I run the way of your commandments, for you enlarge my understanding. Psalm 119:32
8	Jacob Wrestling*	I held him, and would not let him go. Song of Solomon 3:4b
9	The Apostles at Pentecost	O taste and see that the LORD is good; happy are those who take refuge in him. Psalm 34:8*
10	Paul's Mirror Prophecy (1 Cor. 13:12)	Blessed are the pure in heart, for they will see God. Matthew 5:8

Step 1: We are sick with love for God; like Solomon's bride, we yearn only for our beloved groom. All other pleasures lose their appeal in our riveted longing for God.

Step 2: Longing moves into seeking, into a concentrated quest for God. Like Mary Magdalene, who ignored even angels while seeking out Christ, we search through all things, yearning for God alone.

Step 3: Our works for God, though they may be numerous, seem small and inconsequential. Like Jacob, who thought nothing of working fourteen years to win his beloved Rachel, our love for God is such that we would do far more even than this.

Step 4: We have moved through the need for consolation. In accepting anguish, we are energized to serve God with new fervor. Brief respites from the night's barrenness encourage our souls. We are like Peter, whose anguish fueled his swim into Christ's presence.

Step 5: So keen is our desire for union with God that our hearts faint at any delay. Like Rachel, who anguished over her barrenness — "Give me children, or I shall die!" (Genesis 30:1) — our hunger for God gnaws at our souls and will not be appeased.

Step 6: Purified by suffering, our soul races, almost unencumbered, toward God. She has waited on the Lord, who renews her strength, and she rises on strong eagle's wings. We move quickly through this step.

Step 7: Ardor makes us bold in approaching our Lord. Nothing — not another's advice, nor our own shame — will deter us. Like Moses, we stand squarely before God and beg mercy.

Step 8: We long to embrace God for eternity, but we lack the power and readiness for such a union. We are like Jacob clinging to the wrestling "God-man" and Mary Magdalene wrapping arms around the risen Jesus.

Step 9: Like the apostles at Pentecost, God's love burns in our souls. We receive immeasurable treasures in the wake of the fire.

Step 10: After physical death, we unite wholly and rapturously with God. We are, at last, all we were ever meant to be. Paul's mirror prophecy and John of Patmos's divine Revelation hint at the wonder of this glorious uniting.

Resources Cited

 Books and Literature

Albee, Edward. *Who's Afraid of Virginia Woolf?* New York: A Signet Book, 1983.

Austen, Jane. *Pride and Prejudice.* New York: Barnes & Noble Books, 2003.

Bass, Dorothy C., ed. *Practicing Our Faith.* San Francisco: Jossey-Bass, 1997.

The Holy Bible: New International Version. Grand Rapids, MI: Zondervan Bible Publishers, 1978.

Brontë, Charlotte and Emily. *The Works of Charlotte and Emily Brontë.* Charlotte Brontë. *Jane Eyre.* Longmeadow Press, 1981.

Bunyan, John. *Pilgrim's Progress.* Old Tappan, NJ: Fleming H. Revell Co., 1973.

Chittister, Joan, OSB. *Wisdom Distilled from the Daily.* San Francisco: HarperSanFrancisco, 1984.

Cross, St. John of the. *Dark Night of the Soul.* Trans. Mirabai Starr. New York: Riverhead Books, 2002.

Cross, St. John of the. "The Ascent of Mount Carmel." *John of the Cross: Selected Writings.* Ed. Dieran Kavanaugh, OCD. New York: Paulist Press, 1987.

Dickens, Charles. *A Christmas Carol. Charles Dickens Anthology.* New York: Barnes & Noble, 1992.

Edwards, Tilden. *Spiritual Director, Spiritual Companion.* New York: Paulist Press, 2001.

Frankl, Viktor E. *Man's Search for Meaning.* New York: Washington Square Press/Pocket Books, 1984.

Friedman, Edwin H. *Friedman's Fables.* New York: Guilford Press, 1990.

Goudge, Elizabeth. *The Scent of Water.* New York: Coward-McCann, Inc., 1963.

Guenther, Margaret. *Holy Listening.* Cambridge: Cowley Publications, 1992.

Hardy, Richard P. *Search for Nothing: The Life of John of the Cross.* New York: Crossroad, 1982.

Hurnard, Hannah. *Hinds, Feet on High Places.* Wheaton, IL: Tyndale House Publ., 1975.

Kelsey, Morton T. *Companions on the Inner Way: The Art of Spiritual Guidance.* New York: Crossroad, 1996.

Lawrence, Brother. *The Practice of the Presence of God.* Uhrichsville, OH: Barbour Publishing, Inc. 1998.

Leech, Kenneth. *Soul Friend.* San Francisco: HarperSanFrancisco, 1980.

L'Engle, Madeleine. *A Ring of Endless Light.* New York: Laurel-Leaf Books, 1980.

———. *Two-Part Invention: The Story of a Marriage.* San Francisco: HarperSan-Francisco, 1988.

———. *Walking on Water: Reflections on Faith and Art.* Wheaton, IL: Harold Shaw Publishers, 1972.

———. *The Time Quartet.* New York: Farrar, Straus & Giroux, 2003.

Lewis, C. S. *A Grief Observed.* New York: Seabury Press, 1961.

———. *Reflections on the Psalms.* New York: Harcourt Brace Jovanovich, 1958.

———. *Surprised by Joy.* San Diego: Harcourt Brace Jovanovich, 1956.

———. *The Magician's Nephew.* Vol. 1 of *The Chronicles of Narnia.* New York: HarperCollins, 1983.

———. *The Lion, the Witch, and the Wardrobe.* Vol. 2 of *The Chronicles of Narnia.* New York: HarperCollins, 1978.

———. *The Horse and His Boy.* Vol. 3 of *The Chronicles of Narnia.* New York: HarperCollins, 1982.

———. *Prince Caspian.* Vol. 4 of *The Chronicles of Narnia.* New York: Harper-Collins, 1979.

———. *The Voyage of the Dawn Treader.* Vol. 5 of *The Chronicles of Narnia.* New York: HarperCollins, 1980.

———. *The Silver Chair.* Vol. 6 of *The Chronicles of Narnia.* New York: Harper-Collins, 1981.

———. *The Last Battle.* Vol. 7 of *The Chronicles of Narnia.* New York: Harper-Collins, 1984.

MacDonald, George. *Lilith: A Romance.* Grand Rapids, MI: Wm. B. Eerdmans, 1981.

May, Gerald, M.D. *Addiction and Grace.* San Francisco: HarperSanFrancisco, 1988.

———. *Care of Mind: Care of Spirit.* San Francisco: HarperSanFrancisco, 1992.

———. *The Dark Night of the Soul: A Psychiatrist Explores the Connection between Darkness and Spiritual Growth.* San Francisco: HarperSanFrancisco, 2004.

Michael, Chester P., and Marie C. Norrisey. *Prayer and Temperament.* Charlottesville, VA: The Open Door, 1991.

Miller, Calvin. *The Singer.* Downers Grove, IL: InterVaristy Press, 1975.

Mitchell, Margaret. *Gone with the Wind.* New York: Pocket Books, 1969.

Muller, Wayne. *Sabbath.* New York: Bantam Books, 2000.

Norwich, Julian of. *The Revelation of Love in Sixteen Showings.* Trans. M. L. Del Mastro. Liguori, MO: Liguori/Triumph, 1977.

Nouwen, Henri, J. M. *The Return of the Prodigal Son.* New York: Doubleday, 1994.

Paterson, Katherine, retelling. *Parzival.* New York: Puffin Books, 1998.

Raskin, Ellen. *The Westing Game.* New York: Puffin Books, 1992.

Rohr, Richard. *Everything Belongs: The Gift of Contemplative Prayer.* New York: Crossroad, 1999.

Salinger, J. D. *The Catcher in the Rye.* Boston: Little, Brown and Co., 1991.

Sayers, Dorothy L. *Busman's Honeymoon.* New York: Harper & Row, 1986.

———. *Gaudy Night.* New York: Harper & Row, 1986.

———. *Have His Carcase.* New York: Harper & Row, 1986.

———. *Strong Poison.* New York: Harper & Row, 1987.

The Spiritual Formation Bible: New Revised Standard Version. Grand Rapids, MI: Zondervan, 1999.

Tennyson, Alfred Lord."The Crossing of the Bar," 1889. In *The Literature of England,* vol. 2, ed. George K. Anderson and William E. Buckler. Glenview, IL: Scott, Foresman and Company, 1968.

Therese of Lisieux. *Autobiography of St. Therese of Lisieux.* Trans. Ronald Knox. New York: P. J. Kenedy & Sons, 1958.

Tolkein, J. R. R. *The Lord of the Rings.* Boston: Houghton Mifflin Co., 1987.

Von Eschenbach, Wolfram. *Parzival.* Trans. A. T. Hatto. London: Penguin Books, 1980.

Ware, Corinne. *Saint Benedict on the Freeway.* Nashville: Abingdon Press, 2001.

Weil, Simone. *Waiting on God.* USA: Perennial Classics, 2001.

Film

A Beautiful Mind. Directed by Ron Howard, written by Akiva Goldsman. Dreamworks, 2001.

Babette's Feast. Directed by Gabriel Axel, written by Gabriel Axel. Panorama Film International, 1989.

Cast Away. Directed by Robert Zemeckis, written by William Broyles, Jr. Dreamworks, 2000.

Chocolat. Directed by Lasse Hallström, written by Robert Nelson Jacobs. Miramax, 2000.

Contact. Directed by Robert Zemeckis, written by Carl Sagan. Warner Brothers, 1997.

The Elephant Man. Directed by David Lynch, written by Christopher De Vore, Ellen Bergren and David Lynch. Paramount Pictures, 1980.

The Emperor's Club. Directed by Michael Hoffman, written by Neil Tolkin. Universal Pictures, 2002.

Fiddler on the Roof. Directed by Norman Jewison, written by Joseph Stein. Metro Goldwin Mayer, 1971.

Footloose. Directed by Herbert Ross, written by Dean Pitchford. Paramount Pictures, 1984.

Gosford Park. Directed by Robert Altman, written by Julian Fellowes. USA Films, 2001.

The Hours. Directed by Stephen Daldry, written by David Hare. Paramount Pictures and Miramax Films, 2002.

It's a Wonderful Life. Directed by Frank Capra, written by Philip Van Doren Stern, Frances Goodrich, Albert Hackett, Frank Capra, Jo Swerling, and Michael Wilson. Goodtimes™ Home Video Corp., 1946.

Joan of Arcadia. Produced by Barbara Hall. Paramount, 2003–2004.

The Karate Kid. Directed by John G. Avildsen, written by Robert Mark Kamen. Columbia Pictures, 1984.

The Lord of the Rings. Directed by Peter Jackson, written by Fran Walsh, Philippa Boyens, and Peter Jackson. *The Fellowship of the Ring.* New Line Cinema, 2001.

——. *The Return of the King.* Directed by Peter Jackson, written by Fran Walsh, Philippa Boyens, and Peter Jackson. New Line Cinema, 2003.

——. *The Two Towers.* Directed by Peter Jackson, written by Fran Walsh, Philippa Boyens, Stephen Sinclair, and Peter Jackson. New Line Cinema, 2002.

A Man for All Seasons. Directed by Fred Zinnemann, written by Robert Bolt. Columbia Pictures, 1966.

Mystery! Cadfael PBS. Directed by Sebastian Graham Jones and Ken Grieve, written by Simon Burke and Christopher Russell.1994–1998.

Ordinary People. Directed by Robert Redford, written by Alvin Sargent and Nancy Dowd. Paramount, 1980.

The Passion of the Christ. Directed by Mel Gibson, written by Benedict Fitzgerald and Mel Gibson. Twentieth Century Fox, 2004.

The Point. Directed by Fred Wolf, written by Harry Nilsson, Carole Beers, and Norm Lenzer. BMG Video, 1971.

Regarding Henry. Directed by Mike Nichols, written by J. J. Abrams. Paramount Pictures, 1991.

A River Runs Through It. Directed by Robert Redford, written by Richard Friedenberg. Columbia Pictures, 1992.

The Seventh Seal. Directed by Ingmar Bergman, written by Ingmar Bergman. Janus Films, 1957.

Shadowlands. Directed by Richard Attenborough, written by William Nicholson. Savoy, 1993.

The Shawshank Redemption. Directed by Frank Darabont, written by Frank Darabont. Castle Rock Entertainment, 1994.

Star Wars I-VI. Directed by George Lucas, Irvin Kershner, and Richard Marquand, written by George Lucas. Lucas Films, 1977–2005.

Valley of the Dolls. Directed by Mark Robson, written by Helen Deutsch, Dorothy Kingsley, and Jacqueline Susann. Twentieth Century Fox, 1967.

What Dreams May Come. Directed by Vincent Ward, written by Ronald Bass. Polygram Video, 1998.

What's Eating Gilbert Grape. Directed by Lasse Hallström, written by Peter Hedges. Paramount, 1993.

Wild Strawberries. Directed by Ingmar Bergman, written by Ingmar Bergman. Svensk Filmindustries, 1957.

♫ *Music*

American Spiritual, arranged by Burleigh, Harry Thacker. "Sometimes I Feel Like a Motherless Child," circa 1866–1949.

American Spiritual, arranged by Dawson, William Levi. "Jesus Walked that Lonesome Valley," circa 1899–1990.

Armstrong, Billie Joe. "Boulevard of Broken Dreams." Performed by Green Day, *American Idiot* Reprise/WEA, 2004.

Boublil, Alain, and Claude-Michael Schönberg. "Bring Him Home." *Les Misérables* Decca, U.S., 1985.

——. "Finale." *Les Misérables* Decca, U.S., 1985.

Card, Michael, and Phil Naish. "The Edge." Performed by Michael Card, *Poiema* Sparrow/EMD, 1994.

Card, Michael. "Things We Leave Behind." Performed by Michael Card, *Poiema* Sparrow/EMD, 1994.

——. "The Wilderness." Performed by Michael Card, *Ancient Faith* Sparrow Records, 1998.

Coffin, G., and C. King. "Hi-De-Ho That Old Sweet Roll." Performed by Blood, Sweat and Tears, *What Goes Up: The Best of Blood, Sweat and Tears* Sony, 1995.

Cowan, Jim. "When It's All Been Said and Done." Performed by Robin Mark, *Revival in Belfast* Sony, 2002.

De Burgh, Chris. "Don't Pay the Ferryman." Performed by Chris De Burgh, *The Getaway* Universal International, 1982.

Dorsey, Thomas, and George Allen. "Precious Lord, Take My Hand." Hill & Range Songs, Inc., 1938.

Francisco, Don. "He's Alive!" Alexandria, IN: Alexandria House, 1977.

Gaultney, Barbara Fowler. "My Lord Is Near Me All the Time," Broadman Press, 1960.

Hartman, Bob. "Graverobber." *The Petra Youth Choir Collection.* Arranged and compiled by John Lee. Houston, TX: Star Song, 1984.

Hayward, Justin. "Nights in White Satin." Performed by the Moody Blues. *This Is the Moody Blues* Polygram International, 1974.

———. "Question." Performed by the Moody Blues. *This Is the Moody Blues* Polygram International, 1974.

Henley, Don, and Glenn Frey. "Desperado." Performed by the Eagles. *Desperado* Asylum Records, 1973.

Hudson, Mike. "Road to Zion." *The Petra Youth Choir Collection* Arranged and compiled by John Lee. Houston, TX: Star Song, 1984.

Lennon, John. "Beautiful Boy/Darling Boy." Performed by John Lennon, *Double Fantasy* Capital, 1980.

Lennon, John, and Paul McCartney. "Eleanor Rigby." Performed by The Beatles, *Revolver* Capitol, 1966.

———. "Blackbird." Performed by The Beatles, *The White Album* Capital, 1968.

Mark, Robin. "Revival." Performed by Robin Mark, *Revival in Belfast* Sony, 2002.

Newton, John, "Amazing Grace," circa 1725–1807, stanza 5 anonymous, 1790.

Pachelbel, Johann. "Pachelbel's Canon," circa 1680.

Page, Jimmy, and Robert Plant. "Stairway to Heaven." Performed by Led Zeppelin. *How the West Was Won* Rhino/WEA, 1997.

Rice, Tim, and Andrew Lloyd Webber. "Gethsemane." *Jesus Christ Superstar* Decca US, 1970.

Schwartz, Stephen. "Day by Day." *Godspell* Arista, 1971.

Simon, Paul. "The Sound of Silence." Performed by Simon and Garfunkel. *The Graduate* Sony, 1968.

Slick, John. "Not by Sight." *The Petra Youth Choir Collection.* Arranged and compiled by John Lee. Houston, TX: Star Song, 1984.

Stanphill, Ira. "I Know Who Holds Tomorrow." Performed by D. E. Adams. *Songs & Hymns* 1983.

Tallis, Thomas, and Thomas Ken. "Tallis Canon," 1557.

Watts, Isaac. "When I Survey the Wondrous Cross," 1707.

Weiss, George David, and Bob Thiele. "What a Wonderful World," 1967. Arranged by Calvin Custer, performed by Louis Armstrong.

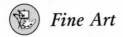 *Fine Art*

Bernini, Gian Lorenzo. *The Ecstasy of St. Teresa.* S. Maria della Vittoria, Rome, 1645–52.

Caravaggio, Michelangelo Merisi da, *The Supper at Emmaus.* National Gallery, London, 1601.

Da Vinci, Leonardo. *Mona Lisa,* The Louvre, Paris, France, 1503.

Degas, Edgar. *The Glass of Absinthe.* Musée d'Orsay, Paris, France, 1876.

Donatello. *The Magdalen in Penitence.* Museo dell Opera dell' Duomo, Florence, Italy, circa 1430–50.

El Greco, *View of Toledo.* Metropolitan Museum of Art, New York, 1610.

———. *The Burial of Count Orgaz.* Church of Santo Tomé, Toledo, 1586.

Friedrich, Caspar David. *The Wanderer in the Mists.* Fine Arts Museum, Hamburg, Germany, 1818.

Grünewald, Matthias. *Isenheim Altarpiece.* Musée d'Unterlinden, Colmar, France, 1510–15.

Hokusai, Katsushika. *The Great Wave.* Honolulu Academy of Arts, Honolulu, Hawaii, 1831.

Lange, Dorothea. *Migrant Mother.* Washington, D.C.: Library of Congress, 1936.

Matisse, Henri. *The Dance.* The Hermitage, St. Petersburg, Russia, 1910.

Michelangelo. *Pietà.* Saint Peter's, Vatican, Rome, 1500.

Millet, Jean-François. *The Gleaners.* Musée d'Orsay, Paris, France, 1857.

Munch, Edvard. *The Scream.* Nasjonal-Galleriet, Oslo, Norway, 1893.

O'Keeffe, Georgia. *Black Iris, III.* Metropolitan Museum of Art, New York, 1926.

Picasso, Pablo. *Guernica.* Museo del Prado, Madrid, Spain, 1937.

Puget, Pierre. *Milo of Crotona.* The Louvre, Paris, France, 1670–82.

Rembrandt. *The Return of the Prodigal.* The Hermitage, St. Petersburg, Russia, 1662.

Soord, Alfred. *The Lost Sheep.* circa 1869–1901.

van Gogh, Vincent. *The Starry Night.* Museum of Modern Art, New York, 1889.

———. *At Eternity's Gate* (or *Worn Out*). van Gogh Museum, Amsterdam, 1882.

Acknowledgments

My thanks to Dr. Corinne Ware, whose teaching fills every page of this book, whose counsel produced its title, and whose determined belief in the need for such a work kept me keeping on. Thanks to Dr. Janettee Henderson, who hoped for me — and for this book — when I could not hope for myself. She is the major contributor for Appendix B. Thanks to Kathleen Davis Niendorff, my agent, whose determination to see this book in print outdistanced my own. And thanks to senior editor Roy M. Carlisle of The Crossroad Publishing Company, who believed enough in an unknown to recommend this work. Gratitude as well to the Episcopal Theological Seminary of the Southwest, whose library I plumbed in researching this book, with a special thanks to Dr. Alan Gregory, whose passion for great literature is contagious. Many, many thanks to my dear friend and soul mate, Jill Coy, who happily reads everything I send her, this book included. I am indebted to Kimberly Ann Owczarski and Ginger Geyer for their Lifeline suggestions. You enriched this book immeasurably.

Deepest gratitude to my husband, David, my merciless editor and dearest friend, and to my daughters, Bethany and Arielle, whose help with and delight in this book's publication is a reward in itself. God's blessings on you all!

About the Author

Kaye P. McKee lives in Austin, Texas, with her husband, David, and daughters, Arielle and Bethany. Kaye, an ordained minister, writer, conference leader, and spiritual director, has earned a master's degree in religious education and a master's in pastoral ministry. She is currently working toward a doctorate in ministry at Austin Presbyterian Seminary. *When God Walks Away* is written following her dark night of several years' duration, endured through God's grace and a quirky sense of humor.

A Word
from the Editor

Every generation must do what Kaye has done in writing this book. And at the same time every generation resists having the gospel, its witness to a God beyond our imagination, and its attendant spirituality spelled out afresh for fear someone, like Kaye, will get it wrong. But Kaye doesn't get it "wrong" and as you will so easily ascertain from reading this book, she gets "it" very right. The "it" is, of course, a new way of seeing an old reality. The reality of how God shows up in an individual life, or seemingly not, as the case may be.

I am not even sure Kaye understood the daunting reality of how to accomplish her task at first. She knew what she wanted to write about, and she had written parts of her story and even tried to do it in a context that would help make sense of it for others. But such is the hubris of us editors; I had a vision for this story to be told in a larger way. The working out of my editorial vision, of course, depends entirely upon whether the writer and editor can agree that it is worth collaborating on. And it also, more importantly, depends upon whether I am seeing something that is already there in the person and the writing or whether I am blindly fantasizing. In this case I was pretty sure that Kaye had more to offer her readers than she even knew. It is with great pleasure and a bit of hubris that I announce that I was right. This book is a wonder to me. As is so often the case, Kaye's ultimate vision was even clearer than my own, and her ability to portray it was skillful.

In light of that allow me to remind you of a few important elements that go into a book such as this. First, you have to have the emotional courage to bare your own soul. As you have seen from reading this book Kaye has done that with candor and humor. Second, you have to believe that you really can illuminate a path or story or in this case, a well-known spiritual treatise, in a unique way. Again Kaye has stepped right up to her marks and done that. Third, you must be willing to submit to the process that God is orchestrating with humility and perseverance. Again, Kaye gets high marks, at least from me, her editor, and hopefully from you, her reader. This combination of candor, courage, and humility is rare. It is what every editor is looking for in the writers that come to him or her for help. It is what makes a book like this one a gem of inestimable value.

Ultimately, and I say this with some trepidation, it is this combination of values and virtues within a writer that help them actually part the veil for us to see spiritual reality in all of its terrifying splendor and loving energy. In other words we see the face and Spirit of God at work. Stop right there, take a deep breath, and tell me that is not what you have wanted all of your life! Now you know why Kaye writes and I publish books. No more, no less.

Roy M. Carlisle
Senior Editor

Of Related Interest

Lyn Doucet and Robin Hebert
WHEN WOMEN PRAY
Our Personal Stories of Extraordinary Grace

"We are two ordinary women who, through God's grace, have had extraordinary experiences of prayer. In this book we share several of these experiences. We have no final answers about God, for in prayer we have experienced God as a beautiful dance of mystery. And yet . . . we know that in the presence of this dance of love we have been transformed. And we now desire to invite you into this sacred dance of daily communion with God." Includes original prayers and helpful tips for praying.

0-8245-2279-6, $16.95, paperback

Leslie Williams, Ph.D.
WHEN WOMEN BUILD THE KINGDOM
Who We Are, What We Do, and How We Relate

These women's stories show how they minister differently from men — how they use their relationships, hearts, and spirituality to build community, how they bring compassion to justice, peace to difficult and violent situations, and authentic spiritual experience to all that they do and are.

0-8245-2363-6, $17.95, paperback

crossroad

Of Related Interest

Paula D'Arcy
WHEN PEOPLE GRIEVE
The Power of Love in the Midst of Pain

Since the publication of her first bestseller *Song for Sarah,* Paula D'Arcy has become an internationally renowned expert in grief and bereavement issues. Now in a completely revised and updated version of an earlier book, Paula helps us understand how to cope with the process of grief and also how to reach out to others in the pain of grief. This classic manual is full of practical advice.

Paula D'Arcy, author of the bestsellers *Gift of the Red Bird* and *Sacred Threshold,* is a former psychotherapist and president of the Red Bird Foundation. She is a frequent speaker in Europe and the United States and lives in northern California.

0-8245-2339-3, $14.95, paperback

Check your local bookstore for availability.
To order directly from the publisher,
please call 1-800-707-0670 for Customer Service
or visit our Web site at *www.cpcbooks.com.*
For catalog orders, please send your request to the address below.

THE CROSSROAD PUBLISHING COMPANY
16 Penn Plaza, Suite 1550
New York, NY 10001

All prices subject to change.

crossroad